VANCOUVER
THEN & NOW

A MAN SITS ALONE WITH A BOOK, THE WHOLE WORLD AROUND HIM GROWS SILENT, A VOICE SO SECRET IT CAN'T BE HEARD, JUST FELT,
IS WHISPERING TO HIM AND LEADING HIM DEEP INTO THE WORLD OF THE GREATEST WONDER AND POWER - HIS OWN IMAGINATION.
MORLEY CALLAGHAN

MAGIC LIGHT PUBLISHING, OTTAWA

VANCOUVER
THEN & NOW

By: Chuck Davis
Photography: John McQuarrie

Published by: Magic Light Publishing
                  John McQuarrie Photography
                  192 Bruyere Street
                  Ottawa, Ontario
                  K1N 5E1

                  (613) 241-1833
                  FAX: 241-2085
                  e-mail: mcq@magma.ca
Corporate orders: (800) 843-0908

Design: John McQuarrie
Production   Kristopher Maxwell
Printing: Book Art Inc., Toronto
Film: Digital Prepress & Printing Professional Ltd
                  Hong Kong

National Library of Canada Cataloguing in Publication Data

Davis, Chuck, 1935-
  Vancouver Then & Now

ISBN 1-894673-08-5

1. Vancouver (B.C.)—History—Pictorial works.
I. McQuarrie, John, 1946- II. Title.

FC3847.37.D374 2001   971.1'33'00222   C2001-901930-0
F1089.5.V22D394 2001

Printed and bound in Hong Kong, China

CONTENTS

View to the Northeast from atop the Guinness Building, over the Marine Building to Canada Place. 2001

In The Beginning

HERE IS HISTORY IN THE MAKING. IT'S JUNE 13, 1792 AND, AS DRAMATICALLY PORTRAYED IN THIS JIM MCKENZIE PAINTING, TWO WORLDS ARE MEETING FOR THE FIRST TIME. WE SEE HERE THE ARRIVAL IN OUR WATERS OF CAPT. GEORGE VANCOUVER ABOARD HMS *DISCOVERY*, WITH HMS *CHATHAM*, HER SMALLER ARMED ESCORT (UNDER WILLIAM BROUGHTON), NOT FAR BEHIND. THIS WAS VANCOUVER'S FIRST COMMAND, AND HE PERFORMED IT EXCEPTIONALLY WELL: THE CHARTS HE MADE OF THE COAST ARE SO GOOD THEY COULD BE USED TODAY.

Vancouver, 34, had several assignments to perform during his 1792 voyage of exploration; the one we're most interested in required him to make a detailed survey of the North American coast from California to Alaska. Because he was also searching for the elusive Northwest Passage Vancouver decided to trace every single mile of the continental shore! The two larger ships were too unwieldy for detailed exploration, so at times Vancouver would get into the *Discovery's* yawl and, with Lt. Peter Puget in a smaller launch (like a big rowboat) tagging along, explore the shore in detail. Their explorations eventually brought them to what we now call the First Narrows. As they passed through the narrows they were met by about 50 native people in canoes, "who conducted themselves," Vancouver later wrote, "with the greatest decorum and civility, presenting us with fish cooked and undressed… resembling smelt." (These were eulachon, or candlefish, so called because they were so rich in oil the natives used them as candles.) Now they entered into an inlet that Vancouver named Burrard's Channel. (Harry Burrard was a naval friend of Vancouver's in England.) It was June 13, 1792.

The captain and his men thoroughly explored the "channel" (and some slept overnight on the ground on the south bank opposite the entrance to Indian Arm). Vancouver could not have had the slightest inkling that a major city would one day occupy that place, and that it would be named in his honour.

A land may be said to be discovered the first time a European, preferably an Englishman, sets foot on it.

Vilhjalmur Stefansson

The explorer made that comment in 1964, articulating the cruel irony in European claims to "discovery" of lands occupied for millennia by other people.

Old people say Indians see first whiteman up near Squamish. When they see first ship they think it an island with three dead trees…Indian braves in about twenty canoes come down Squamish River, go see. Get nearer, see men on island, men have black clothes with high hat coming to point at top…

August Jack Khahtsahlano, quoted in J.S. Matthews, Early Vancouver, volume 2, number 37.

Captain Vancouver, 1792 by Jim McKenzie

Capt. Vancouver would be thunderstruck to see what this corner of the Pacific Coast looks like today, and to learn that the important and spectacularly attractive city on this site had been named for him... particularly when we learn he was dismayed to discover he was not the first European to see this spot. Eight days after he had explored "Burrard's Channel," returning to the area after exploring what he named Howe Sound close up, Vancouver was startled–and dismayed–to find two Spanish ships moored off Point Grey. They were commanded by Dionisio Alcala-Galiano in the brig *Sutil* and Cayetano Valdes in the schooner *Mexicana*. Spain and England had competing claims to the area and, in fact, another of Vancouver's assignments was to go to Nootka on Vancouver Island and meet there with a Spanish representative to negotiate a surrender of the Spanish claims. He was even more dismayed to discover that another Spaniard, Jose Maria Narvaez, had been in these same waters almost exactly a year earlier. (Yes, the first European to see the future site of our city was a Spaniard.) Vancouver named Spanish Banks in tribute to his new friends.

A word about his little ships. HMS *Discovery* was not much more than 30 metres long, the *Chatham* was less than 17. All available space aboard the ships was used for equipment and crews' quarters. Fresh water and food had to be acquired along the route. For these men in 1792, it has been written, "sustaining life was more time-consuming than their mission of mapping these uncharted waters." There were 100 crew jammed into Discovery, and they lived under those conditions for more than four years. (The two ships left Falmouth April 1, 1791 and returned in October, 1795.) Vancouver's brief stay had a profound resolution: in his wake would rise a modern metropolitan area with more than two million residents.

We need the West coast. It is the psychological equivalent of a black satin negligee, the little luxury we allow ourselves when we're weary of wearing practical cotton pyjamas. It is the sandbox in the Canadian schoolyard. It is the escape valve for an entire country.

PAUL GRESCOE, journalist, "Coasting" The Canadian Magazine, May 25th, 1975)

Aerial view looking east over Stanley Park to Vancouver, 2001.

Moodyville Mill, 1870. Vancouver Public Library / 003392

MOODYVILLE

It was 1862, exactly 70 years after George Vancouver had explored Burrard Inlet, before Europeans returned. It was wood that brought them. The giant trees of southwestern British Columbia were, to use a current term of approval, awesome. After being felled, one typical specimen was measured at 91 metres (300 feet), about the height of the Marine Building. One of the mills that sprang up quickly after the arrival of Europeans was on the north shore of the Inlet. By 1864 Pioneer Mills was shipping wood to Adelaide, Australia, the first export to a foreign port from Burrard Inlet.

The mill didn't really thrive until a savvy, Maine-born lumberman named Sewell Moody bought it in 1865. "Sew" Moody was a tough and able administrator. He allowed no liquor in the area, and his thirsty workers would have to go all the way to New Westminster until 1867, when they could row across to the south shore and buy a drink at Gassy Jack Deighton's saloon in Gastown. The area around Moody's mill began to be called Moodyville. If you stood in Gassy Jack's with a beer in your hand in 1870, gazing across the inlet, Moodyville would have looked as above…although perhaps not as clear. (Moody himself shunned the town: he lived in Victoria.) In February of 1882 electric lights were installed at the mill so work could carry on into the night. These were the first electric lights north of San Francisco, and all the locals came around to see. The mayor and council of Victoria made a special trip over to have a look at this modern marvel. And a gasp of wonder arose from the assembled crowd when suddenly, at the flick of a switch, artificial light flooded the scene.

But that was just a small example of the wonders that were to come.

Dock area of North Vancouver just to the west of the Second Narrows Bridge, as viewed from New Brighton Park in Vancouver. The old Moodyville Mill was located just to the right of the grain elevators near the intersection of today's Low Level and Cotton Roads.

Moodyville Mill, much expanded from the time of the photograph on the opposite page, 1898.
Vancouver Public Library / 000013

Hastings Mill, located on the site of present-day Centennial Pier at the foot of Dunlevy Street in Vancouver, 1900. The Mission Reserve and St Pauls Church (still there today just west of Lonsdale) on the north shore, are dimly visible through the smoke of the mill. Vancouver Public Library / 019776

The sidewheeler Princess Louise at the Hastings Mill Dock in 1886. Vancouver Public Library / 000505

Sailing ships waiting to load at Hastings Mill, 1888. National Archives of Canada / C 020865

Hastings Mill Store Museum, Kitsilano Beach Park, 2001.

The transition from sail to steam is evident in this 1919 photograph. While sailing ships still dock at the mill, the steam-powered vessels crossing Burrard Inlet provide graphic evidence of the end of an era. Vancouver Public Library / 003639

View of Centennial Pier area from Portside Park at the foot of Main Street, 2001.

Where Hastings Mill once stood we now have the ceaseless activity of Canada's largest port. The huge container cranes of Centennial Pier tower overhead and just to the west the sail-like silhouette of Canada Place reminds us of the bygone age of sail that dominated early Burrard Inlet.

HASTINGS MILL

The change here since June 1867, when Hastings Mill was first built at what is now the north foot of Dunlevy Street, is stunning. Look at that little inset picture on the left of the opposite page, which shows the mill area nearly 20 years after it began operating, then look at Centennial Pier today (above). It was British financing that made the mill possible, and brought this first industry to the south shore of Burrard Inlet—where the city of Vancouver would eventually rise.

And it was this mill and her thirsty workers that lured John "Gassy Jack" Deighton to the area. The manager who succeeded the curmudgeonly Edward Stamp, J.A. Raymur, delivered himself of one of the city's great quotes when he took over. The mill and its surroundings had become squalid and unkempt, and when Raymur first surveyed it he was livid. "What," he asked, "is the meaning of this aggregation of filth?" He cleaned it up fast. (He also, in 1869, gave his employees a library.)

By 1919, as that remarkable photograph to the left indicates, Hastings Mill had grown enormously. But today, nothing of it remains except for a tiny store that once sold dry goods to the workers and their families. On July 28, 1930 the Hastings Mill Store was moved by barge from this area to the north foot of Alma Street in Kitsilano, and "gently set down among the flowers." It became a museum, (inset, facing page) operated by the Native Daughters of British Columbia.

Aerial view to the south over Burrard Inlet.

Bird's eye view of Vancouver, 1898 City of Vancouver Archives / Map 547

The city's population has grown to about 25,000, and its southern boundary is at West 16th Avenue. (Beyond lay the big, sprawling and sparsely settled municipality of South Vancouver.) Note how far east False Creek extends and note, too, the mix of sailing and steam ships in Coal Harbour. New arrivals to the city this year: Canada's first permanent movie theatre, the *Province* newspaper and pay telephones (5 cents) at English Bay.

Bird's eye view of Vancouver 1908, National Archives of Canada / 005991

TURN OF THE CENTURY

It's 10 years later, sailing ships have disappeared, new bridges have been built, and our population is pushing 100,000. The Vancouver of 1908 now has a stock exchange, and two new neighbors—the City of North Vancouver, incorporated in 1907 after splitting from North Vancouver District, and the Municipality of Point Grey, newly seceded from the Municipality of South Vancouver. Holy Rosary Church has begun services (it will later be designated a cathedral), and now there's a regular scheduled ferry service to the north shore. Woodward's and Spencer's have started their respective department stores, the Carnegie Library is luring readers at Main and Hastings, and a tourist bus service has started in Stanley Park. Also new: a gas station, the first in Canada, at the southeast corner of Smithe and Cambie Streets. The station's "tank" is a converted water heater, the hose is an ordinary garden hose, and the attendant sits outside on a kitchen chair. At first, a busy morning sees three automobiles filling up.

How could such bird's-eye views—hugely popular in Canada and the U.S. around the turn of the century—be obtained in the days before flight? "Preparation of panoramic maps," says the Library of Congress, "involved a vast amount of painstakingly detailed labor. For each project a frame or projection was developed, showing in perspective the pattern of streets. The artist then walked in the street, sketching buildings, trees, and other features to present a complete and accurate landscape as though seen from an elevation of 2,000 to 3,000 feet… Panoramic maps graphically depict the vibrant life of a city. Harbors are shown choked with ships, often to the extent of constituting hazards to navigation. Trains speed along railroad tracks, at times on the same roadbed with locomotives and cars headed in the opposite direction. People and horsedrawn carriages fill the streets, and smoke belches from the stacks of industrial plants."

First CPR Station at the foot of Howe Street. Vancouver Public Library / 001092

First Train in Vancouver

From early morning yesterday it was easy to see that some unusual occurrence was about to take place. The streets were covered with people many in holiday costumes walking around watching the work of decorating…The building …along the principal streets were decorated with evergreens, flags, bunting etc., while from every flagmast in the city a flag of some nationality was flying out before the breeze… All the ships in harbor were decked out in all colors…The scene at the station was a very lively and enthusiastic one, the roadway, wharf, platform and the bank above were covered with people waiting the arrival of the train…

At 12.45 while all were straining their eyes eastwards, the loud whistle of the engine was heard, "here she comes"! "here she comes"! was heard on all sides and at the same time a rush for the platform was made by those on the banks above. A minute later amidst the cheers of the people, ringing of bells and the shrill cry of the locomotive whistle, the first through passenger train entered the station and pulled up in Vancouver.

From "Ocean to Ocean," *The Daily News-Advertiser, 24 May 1887.*

A Great Day

Electricity was in the air. Everyone in the big crowd gathered on the waterfront this sunny May morning has a sense their lives are about to change forever. But few could anticipate just how sweeping these changes would be. With the arrival of the CPR's first passenger train from far off Montreal, they have become instantly connected to the rest of their vast young country and the world. But could they know that the railway would open their little community to thousands of new inhabitants that would transform their isolated, frontier lumber town of a few thousand people into a thriving city of international importance?

Just a stone's throw from the tiny wooden platform welcoming these first, transcontinental passengers lay the CPR wharves that would become Canada's gateway to the Orient. Sail would soon give way to steam and the CPR's gleaming new Empress liners would become frequent visitors to Burrard Inlet, signaling Vancouver's entry into the excitement of international trade and travel. The economic and cultural boost Vancouverites were about to experience would surpass anything the cheering people in these photographs could possibly imagine. Or could it?

CPR president William Van Horne had strongly (and successfully) recommended the new city be named Vancouver. Van Horne also ensured the railway's terminus would be Coal Harbour, and not Port Moody at the head of Burrard Inlet, the railway's first announced choice. (Ocean-going ships wouldn't have been able to berth at Port Moody.) Once again, Van Horne had shaped the little city's future.

Engine No. 374, which had taken over from another locomotive at Port Moody, 20 kilometres to the east, brought the train in under a giant banner that read: The Occident Greets the Orient. A portrait of Queen Victoria gazed regally down from the little engine's smokestack, and engineer Peter Righter grinned broadly as a brass band struck up a stirring rendition of See, the Conquering Hero Comes.

Vancouver has an understandably fond affection for Engine No. 374, which chugged into town that fateful day. At the end of its useful life, it was shunted unceremoniously off to a remote yard somewhere by the railway. Years later, perhaps realizing the potential value the engine would have for Vancouverites, the railway donated it to the city, which put it on display in a Kitsilano park. Exposed to the elements, old No. 374 sat for years, a giant rusting toy for kids of all ages. Then Evelyn Atkinson stepped in. A lively and dedicated lady, "Evie" founded The Friends of 374, and helped raise $500,000 to restore the engine and find it a new home in The Roundhouse, at the eastern end of Davie Street. (Thousands of people admired the Little Engine that Could when it went on display during Expo 86.) Now beautifully restored by aficionados of old locomotives, No. 374 sits gleaming in its own

glassed-in room where volunteer old timers answer visitors' questions. (Pssst! For technical reasons too detailed to explain here, #374 has been altered slightly from its appearance when it first arrived in Vancouver.)

The first passenger to step down onto the platform, a 22-year-old Welshman named Jonathan Rogers, laughingly admitted later he thought the band was playing for him. ("See, the Conquering Hero comes! Sound the trumpets, beat the drums! Sports prepare, the laurel bring; Songs of triumph to him sing!") Symbolically, Rogers' arrival was perfect: he would become one of the city's major developers, building many of the city's office blocks, including the attractive building named for him and still there at Pender and Granville. His wife Elizabeth, also Welsh-born, would become one of the city's major cultural leaders: the organizing meeting of the Vancouver Art Gallery was held in her living room.

Two young friends enjoy the opportunity to explore the cab of Engine #374 in its beautiful home in the old roundhouse on Davie Street.

The railway made Vancouver, and kept on making it after its 1887 arrival. There were a couple of thousand of us then, but the city began growing so quickly a banner was strung across Granville reading, "In 1910 Vancouver

CPR Station, 1912 Leonard Frank / Vancouver Public Library / 011439

By 1911 the CPR had been in Vancouver for 25 years. Its tax exemption was about to end and, as you can see in this 1912 photo, the railway owned a great deal of land in the downtown. Also, the Panama Canal was scheduled to open in 1914 and the railway expected that to increase its business. To avoid the tax levy and find more useable land they pulled stakes and moved their freight yards and engine facility east to the broad, level land of Port Coquitlam. The results in Vancouver can be seen in the present-day photograph above: that land became available for later developments like the Pan Pacific Hotel, left, the Waterfront Centre Hotel, centre, and the lofty Granville Square office tower, right.

CPR station on Cordova at the foot of Granville in its 21st century incarnation as the SeaBus Terminal, 2001.

The CPR's magnificent Royal Hudson engines were granted that unique "Royal" designation as a result of their excellent service. Engine #2850, shown here at the Canadian Pacific station in 1939 after carrying King George VI and Queen Elizabeth (now the Queen Mother) across the country at high speed and with faultless precision, was one of the last in the series. Canadian Pacific, proud of the machines, asked the King for permission to designate all the locomotives in the series as "Royal." His Majesty was so impressed with them that he immediately agreed. (The royal couple used the same train on the return voyage, but this time via Canadian National's tracks.)

Today, Engine #2860, a sister to this one, takes B.C. Rail passengers from North Vancouver to Squamish in the summer.

Royal Hudson locomotive No. 2860 decked out in her annual "Jingle Bells Express" finery. Every Christmas special runs from North Vancouver to Squamish help Vanvouverites and visitors alike celebrate Christmas in this unique way. Proceeds from these runs go to charity.

Photo Courtesy of B.C. Rail

B.C. Rail's Royal Hudson steaming along the picturesque shoreline of Howe Sound between Squamish and Horseshoe Bay. Photo Courtesy of B.C. Rail

The railway has held us together, spanning a bleak Precambrian desert, an angry ocean of plumed mountains, a chill wasteland of muskeg, to give us unity we could not otherwise have achieved.

Pierre Berton, author and media personality, Maclean's, August 21, 1989

There was a time in this fair land when the railroad did not run,
When the wild majestic mountains stood alone against the sun,
Long before the white man and long before the wheel
When the green dark forest was too silent to be real.

Gordon Lightfoot *These are the opening lines of the composer and singer's moving ballad "Canadian Railroad Trilogy".*

Giant freight train hauling prairie grain south alongside the Thompson River, grain headed for huge bulk carrier ships waiting in the Port of Vancouver. And it is this very same CPR right-of-way that old engine No. 374 took on her historic journey back in 1887.

How pleasant, on a summer's day in 1893, to gather around the little bandshell in "CPR Park" at Georgia and Granville Streets. (Among the musical hits that year: *Oh, Promise Me* and *The June-Bug's Dance*.) City locals and guests in the first Hotel Vancouver, on the right, could stroll around the park, perhaps later succumbing to the allure of the arched portal framing the entrance to the Hudson's Bay department store. This photograph must have been taken on one of Vancouver's 'rare' rainy days! Vancouver Public Library / 000001

There's not a backhoe or a crane or even a horse in sight in this 1886 shot of men clearing the site for the railway's new hotel. This big crew was supplied with little more than picks, axes, shovels and strong backs. Vancouver Public Library / 000055

A tourist poses, dwarfed between two giant trees (near today's Burrard and Robson), with the first Hotel Vancouver peeking out of the mist in the background. Some of these forest titans topped out at well over 300 feet (91 metres). photograph William Notman / Vancouver Public Library / 013009

Georgia Street façade of Hotel Vancouver, 1889 William Notman / Vancouver Public Library / 008623

Elegant lobby of Hotel Vancouver, 1889 Vancouver Public Library / 008625

HOTEL VANCOUVER

THE CPR DEMONSTRATED ITS CONFIDENCE IN THE FUTURE OF A YOUNG VANCOUVER BY BUILDING THIS 60-ROOM HOTEL, HUGE FOR A CITY OF A FEW THOUSAND RESIDENTS THAT ALREADY HAD MORE THAN A DOZEN SMALL HOTELS. IT ROSE RATHER GRANDLY AMID A VAST AND UNSIGHTLY TANGLE OF STUMPS AND BRUSH, A TOUCH OF OLD WORLD ELEGANCE THAT WOWED THE LOCALS . . . PARTICULARLY SINCE THEIR CITY HAD BURNED TO THE GROUND JUST TWO YEARS BEFORE. (THE ORIGINAL PLANS FOR THE HOTEL WERE DESTROYED IN THE GREAT FIRE OF JUNE 13, 1886, AND THE ARCHITECT HAD TO START ALL OVER AGAIN.) THE INTERIOR FITTINGS WERE AS FINE AS ANYTHING ON THE CONTINENT, AS A GAWKING PARADE OF CITIZENS DISCOVERED FOR THEMSELVES.

But the exterior brought its architect, Thomas Sorby, to grief. Shortly after the hotel opened in May, 1888 (not May, 1887 as is often written) the president of the railway, a flinty-eyed pitbull of a man named William Van Horne, arrived in town. Van Horne was at a reception when he was approached by Sorby, who proudly introduced himself as the new hotel's architect. If Sorby was hoping for compliments, he'd come to the wrong man. Van Horne snorted. "Are you the damned fool who put in all those little windows?" he asked. "It looks like a hospital." Sorby's response is not recorded.

Other Vancouverites called the building a "glorified farmhouse," but they soon began to haunt its elegant lobby to enjoy a drink, perhaps a fine cigar and the shiny brass spittoons. Inspired to lively conversation in these rich surroundings they would remain for hours.

(After a time the hotel removed some of its lobby chairs to discourage loiterers.) The best rooms and three good meals cost guests $4 a day.

And why had the C.P.R. erected their showpiece hotel in this remote, tangled spot so far from the busy haunts of Cordova and Water Streets (against the wishes of city council)? Van Horne's intention was to pull the centre of town away from Gastown and toward his hotel, which stood in the midst of vast and valuable tracts of land the railway just happened to own. As they often did for Van Horne, things worked just as he had envisioned. The Hudson's Bay Company opened a lavish new store on Georgia Street, directly opposite the hotel and the die was cast. Before long, a new downtown began to emerge. One man had reshaped the city.

There are no automobiles visible in this charming 1906 image of a wintry Georgia and Granville, even though the first steam-powered car showed up in 1899. Vancouver got its first gasoline-powered machines in 1904 and while the horse would continue to occupy Vancouver's streets for years to come, its days were numbered. Just nudging its way into the picture on the left is one of the B.C. Electric Company's streetcars, running along Granville Street. It wouldn't be long before streetcars, taxis and other automobiles nudged horses right off the city's streets, never to be seen again.

Perhaps the lady in the two-horse open sleigh nearest the camera has come downtown to shop for Christmas gifts. And note the lady in the middle distance pulling her child along on a tiny sled.

A few weeks before this picture was taken, the Hotel Vancouver, on the left, hosted its inaugural luncheon for the Vancouver branch of the Canadian Club. The guest of honor was Governor General Earl Grey, after whom football's most coveted cup and one of the country's favorite teas were named. Vancouver Public Library / 002452

A metropolis of 1.3m people, of innumerable nationalities, [Vancouver] still has the public manners of an English country town half a century ago. It seldom raises its voice. It would not dream of jumping a light…Quiet, frequent, meticulously driven are the buses. Sleek and smooth is the SkyTrain… Majestically accelerates the catamaran SeaBus across the Burrard Inlet. There are taxis especially humped to accommodate wheelchairs in Vancouver, and talking elevators for the blind, and the aerial tramway that runs up to the summit of Grouse Mountain every day is operated by brisk, well-exercised girls of inimaginable helpfulness.

Jan Morris, "Have A Nice Day", Saturday Night, February 1988.

Almost 100 years later the snow is gone and so is absolutely everything visible in the wonderful photograph at left. Pacific Centre occupies the southwest corner of Granville, home to the first two Hotels Vancouver, and the present Hotel Vancouver now sits two blocks to the west of her predecessors.

This fountain now occupies the area in front of the courthouse where the flagpole dominated in the '20s. Pacific Centre now occupies the site of the first two Hotels Vancouver and the present-day hotel is reflected in the black glass of the Toronto- Dominion Bank Building

The glory of the Italian Renaissance found an echo in this spectacular building, the second Hotel Vancouver. Vancouverites loved their new hotel from the moment it opened in 1916. Distinguished guests drove up to the hotel sheltered by a lofty porte-cochere and swept into an elegant lobby where the city's (and the world's) elite were frequently seen. Actress Ethel Barrymore was once spotted smoking a cigar there! A spacious and airy roof garden, 228 feet above the street, was the scene of frequent social gatherings and teas.

I remember one time in the early days of Vancouver when we used to ride on the left side of the road… Nineteen twenty-two they changed over… I remember that Sunday quite well. I went out into the street to watch it happen and everybody drove so carefully, suddenly changing to the other side of the street; there were no accidents at all. One thing it did upset. A corner drugstore that used to be a street car stop would suddenly find itself on the wrong side of the street when they changed the traffic. It upset a lot of shop keepers at various strategic corners that were no longer where the public got on and off.

From library workshop, interview number 179, Oral History Programme, Reynoldston Research and Studies

Hotel Vancouver and Courthouse, c.1925
Vancouver Public Library / 013192

Leonard Frank / Vancouver Public Library / 005919

Sadly, construction flaws and financial rigors imposed by the Great Depression spelled doom for this grand symbol of the gilded age. Replaced in 1939 by the present Hotel Vancouver, she sat gloomily empty for years, finding temporary reprieve as a refuge for homeless veterans of the Second World War, before succumbing to the wrecker's ball in 1949.

Today, hidden in homes all around Greater Vancouver, are mementos of this great hostelry. Wrote the *Province* on January 5, 1949: "Famous bathtubs, which once cradled the shapely limbs of the divine Sarah Bernhardt and the immortal Pavlova, ensconced the muscular torso of the mighty Babe Ruth and immersed the well-padded frame of Winston Churchill will be on sale here shortly."

The 1916 photo above, taken shortly after the hotel's opening, reminds us that traffic once moved on the "wrong" side of the street. (The switch came in January of 1922.) Another vanished landmark, the Birks Building, can be seen behind the hotel in the picture to the left. And traffic now flows on the "right" side. Today, the courthouse is home to the Vancouver Art Gallery.

Woman enjoying the view from roof Garden of the second Hotel Vancouver, C.1935.
Photo courtesy of the Hotel Vancouver.

View of Court House Square and the corner of Georgia and Hornby, August 29th, 1913. Crowds have gathered to witness the erection of the famous Court House flag pole, one of the tallest in the world. Weighing in at a hefty nine tons and reaching up to about 200 feet, the pole stood until 1936 when it was removed after deteriorating to a point that it created a safety hazard. Today's Hotel Vancouver now stands on the vacant lot enclosed by advertising billboards.
City of Vancouver Archives / BU.N.584#1P88

View of Court House Square and the Hotel Vancouver at the corner of Georgia and Hornby, 2001. This photograph was taken from the roof of Pacific Centre which sits on the site of the original two Hotels Vancouver.

Fountain now occupying the site of the famous Court House flagpole. Silhouetted behind the fountain is the old Court House, now home to the Vancouver Art Gallery.

Hotel Vancouver under construction, 1931. Vancouver Public Library / 008909

View north on Granville to Georgia, 1935. Vancouver Public Library / 004323

This was a scene familiar to locals for many years: the third Hotel Vancouver under construction. It took 11 years to complete! Canadian National began building the hotel, which they intended to name the British Columbian, in 1928. They hoped to steal some of rival CPR's business but their timing couldn't have been worse. The ground was barely broken when the Great Depression descended and construction abruptly halted. At the same time, business at the CPR's Hotel Vancouver (from which the photo at upper left was taken—note the hotel's shadow on the courthouse lawn) was slipping. Finally, the two railways came to an agreement by which they would be joint operators of the new "Hotel Vancouver". The existing Hotel Vancouver would be demolished.

Other familiar but now-vanished landmarks can be seen in the same photograph. The white terra-cotta-topped Georgia Medical Dental Building had been standing at the northwest corner of Georgia and Hornby since 1929. Then, one day in 1989, the streets were jammed with observers held behind barricades as the venerable old building was destroyed in a controlled explosion. The huge crowd cheered as the big, handsome building imploded and came thundering down, kicking up a roiling storm of dust that stretched for blocks. A similar explosive ending befell the seven-storey Devonshire Hotel, seen here beside the Georgia Hotel. Fortunately, the Georgia, on the right, and the Marine Building behind it, remain with us today.

Excavation for Hotel Vancouver with Wesley Methodist Church in the background, 1929. Vancouver Public Library / 000030

Hotel Vancouver, 2001

Granville Street (upper right, opposite) in 1935, showing both Hotels Vancouver. The chateau-style hotel, on the left, was still unfinished. This was Depression-era Vancouver, and on one day in April a band of hungry, unemployed men roamed in protest through the Hudson's Bay Store—hidden here by the clock-topped Vancouver Block. By June more local men would board freight trains for the famous "Trek to Ottawa."

Granville was Theatre Row long before it got that nickname. The big sign for one of the many movie houses along the street, the Dominion, was a landmark for years. Some of those people scurrying along the sidewalk down there might well be rushing to see Ginger Rogers and Fred Astaire in a sparkling new hit called Top Hat. Other hit movies in 1935 included: Mutiny on the Bounty, David Copperfield, The Informer, and The Lives of a Bengal Lancer.

The third Hotel Vancouver opened its 550 guest rooms in May, 1939 just in time for a visit by King George VI and Queen Elizabeth (now the Queen Mother). Fittingly, the Royal Couple were the first to enjoy the hotel's lavish, five bedroom Royal Suite.

Hotel Vancouver, 1939 Vancouver Public Library / 025091

VIEW TO GROWTH

Imagine you are a guest of the Hotel Vancouver in the summer of 1888. It's just two years after the fire that virtually wiped Vancouver off the map but, looking out the 4th floor window of your plush suite, you would never know it. The little city is thriving. Returning on business the following year, you request your old room and the view reflects more growth, mostly the stately new homes of Blueblood Alley built on West Hastings for CPR executives. But then - just one year later - Pow! By 1890 (right) Vancouver is firmly launched on a path to growth that will continue unbroken for eight decades. That's the corner of Howe and Georgia, with Howe Street (the future financial heart of the city) running diagonally to the upper right. Now occupying the space of the East India Tea Company is the Georgia Hotel.

View to the north west from the first Hotel Vancouver, 1888 Bailey Brothers / Vancouver Public Library / 013242

View to the north west from the first Hotel Vancouver, 1889 Bailey Brothers / Vancouver Public Library / 019728

View to the north west from the first Hotel Vancouver, 1890   Vancouver Public Library / 019732

DOMINION PHOTO CO.
E.D. 3256

JULY N. 1889

ancouver, circa July 1890, from roof of first Hotel Vancouver, on southwest corner of Granville and Georgia. Wood plank sidewalks. ↑ Granville and Georgia St

| Van Horne Blk. in 1959 called Colonial Theatre. | C.P.R. park | site of Bank of Montreal. In 1959 Imperial | Hudson's Bay uptown store. | New York Blk In 1959, Saba Bros. | One half only of Granville street used as road; other half, small boulders, stones, long grass, weeds. Wood planks between rails. | Site of Hudson's Bay stor Homer St. Methodist Chu L.G.N. 693. Str. P.364. City Archives. g st |

To the left, Dominion Day in 1889 (Canada was 22 years old) finds ships in Burrard Inlet flying ribbons and bunting to mark the holiday. Some of those ships may have brought tea from China, a hot commodity those days. In 1887 the CPR astonished the world by delivering tea from Yokohama, Japan via Vancouver to London, England in just 29 days, when more than 40 days by an all-water route was standard. The city's name as a transshipment point was made. The Moodyville Mill just visible across Burrard Inlet has the north shore pretty much to itself.

A room on the northeast corner of the old Hotel Vancouver would offer a more dramatic vista to the heart of the old and new business districts. Here's what you would have seen in 1890. Dirt roads, wooden sidewalks…and electric streetcars! (We first got electricity in 1887, electric streetcars two years later.) The photographer has captured an unforgettable image: a lone little car clanking its way up toward Georgia Street along a single track down a Granville Street that is still half undone. The streetcar's route took it north on Westminster Avenue (now Main Street), then along Powell, Carrall, Cordova, Cambie, Hastings and Granville to Drake Street. Just as it does today, public transit brought shoppers downtown. In 1893, the three-storey Hudson's Bay moved into the spot it occupies to this day: the lot at the northeast corner of Georgia and Granville. Slowly, steadily, Granville has begun to supplant Hastings as the city's major shopping thoroughfare. That's Homer Street Methodist Church in the right background.

From the window of the brand-new (third and current) Hotel Vancouver a 1939 look to the north gives us our first view of a building still with us today. The Marine Building, architectural icon most associated with Vancouver, had opened in 1930. Its planners had conceived of it as a great crag of a building, "rising from the sea, clinging with sea flora and fauna, in sea-green flashed with gold." Alas, by 2000 (above) this Art Deco masterpiece was almost totally hidden from the same viewpoint by a forest of modern skyscrapers.

Note the floating gas stations, a Coal Harbour fixture since the 1930s. Vancouverites from the earliest days took advantage of the boating opportunities that abound here. Today there are more than 10,000 marina or yacht club berths in Greater Vancouver.

View northwest over Burrard Street to Coal Harbour and the north shore mountains from the Hotel Vancouver, 1939.
Vancouver Public Library I 019742

View to the north west over the corner of Granville and Georgia, 2001.

Aerial view of the central business district from over False Creek, 2001. The north end of the Granville Street Bridge can be seen in the left foreground while the new condo towers and the ongoing development of the old Expo 86 site in Yaletown anchors the right foreground.

Not more than twenty-five cows shall be kept by any one person, family, partnership, company or corporation at any one time within the limits of the city.

By-law number 263, 16 January 1902

While the venerable old Marine Building no longer dominates the Vancouver skyline, she still clings stubbornly to her prize views of Burrard Inlet and Coal Harbour. And she exudes an indefinable panache that sets her apart from the surrounding gaggle of chic glass towers whose main charm lies in their ability to reflect her timeless elegance. This is a bit of a stretch, but if you were a building on New Year's Eve, looking for someone to sign the last dance on your card, who would you be looking to for that midnight waltz? The only way you will understand this question is if you know what a 'dance card' is !!! Not many of us left!

Back in 1970 you could look east (above) and see Canadian Pacific's Pier B-C, gone today to be replaced by the sails of Canada Place (inset facing page). An earlier view to the west (below) shows what you'd have seen from the Marine Building in 1935. The Coal Harbour Seawalk wasn't even a concept in a city planner's dream-book.

If you look closely at the 1970 photo at left you can see the cornice of the Marine Building immediately in front of the photographer's vantage point. This is the only common element connecting the old and new photos on these two pages. The contemporary photos on this page were taken from the Waterfront Centre (below) and the Guinness Building (right). The inset photo reflects the considerable development of the rail lands to the east of the Marine Building since 1970, while the westward view illustrates the dramatic transition Vancouverites can expect in the land reclaimed from Burrard Inlet in the decade to come. In the 2011 edition of this book we'll re-shoot the image below to show you the Marine Building's new neighbours.

View to the northwest over Coal Harbour and Stanley Park to the north shore.

Stanley Park looms in the background of the photo at upper right, taken in 1956. The number of people visiting the park went up that year with the opening of the Vancouver Public Aquarium. But on this side of the park, Georgia Street looks rather unkempt. Five years later, in 1961 (lower right), things have changed with the arrival of the upscale Bayshore Inn. The $6 million hotel, opened March 27, was said to be the most luxurious on the continent. Loony billionaire Howard Hughes stayed here in 1972, and thereby hangs a tale: Vancouver tax expert David Ingram says Hughes left Vancouver (and Canada) on the 181st or 182nd day of his stay, because if he had stayed just one more day, he would have become taxable in Canada on his *total* world income.

Today, the much expanded Westin Bayshore anchors a lot of new development on Coal Harbour, and a long shoreside promenade gives West End strollers unmatched views of the park, the inlet and the north shore mountains.

Early morning calm of Coal Harbour Quay.

GASTOWN

View west along Water Street and its famous steam clock at the corner of Cambie, 2000.

WELCOME TO DOWNTOWN VANCOUVER, 1884. ACTUALLY, THIS HOMELY LITTLE LINE OF BUILDINGS WAS OFFICIALLY CALLED GRANVILLE TOWNSITE BACK THEN, FOR THE COLONIAL SECRETARY OF THE TIME, AND EVEN THAT WAS A FORMAL NAME THAT NOT ALL THE LOCALS USED. TO THEM, IT WAS GASTOWN. THAT'S WATER STREET ALONG WHICH THOSE BUILDINGS ARE ARRAYED, AND NOTE THEY ALL FACE BURRARD INLET. THE PHOTOGRAPHER, PERHAPS HARRY DEVINE, STOOD ON A PIER OUT OVER THE WATER AND RECORDED FOR US, MORE THAN 115 YEARS LATER, THE VERY BEGINNINGS OF OUR CITY.

Back in the woods there you'd find a broad road—little more than a rough path carved out between lofty trees—that led you 12 kilometres away to the city of New Westminster.

Join us now for a stroll down Water Street, the town's major thoroughfare, and let's see who's home. By the way, when the tide is out Gastown is high and dry, when it's in the buildings jut out over the water. That makes it easier to bring in supplies, which virtually all come in by water, some brought by local native people in canoes. Bigger boats tie up against the floats you see in the foreground.

The two-storey peaked building on the left with the men standing on the second-floor verandah is the Sunnyside Hotel, a relative old-timer here, built around 1876. Sewage from the hotel (and everywhere else in town) was dumped directly into the inlet. It was a good idea to hold off on trips to the toilet until the tide was in! There was no running water, and electricity wouldn't arrive for three years yet, so guests were supplied with oil lamps. Joe Fortes, the famous English Bay lifeguard, worked here as a bartender.

The long float in the foreground was the Sunnyside's, and boats like the Beaver tied up here when bringing in food and fuel and newcomers. Constable Jonathan Miller, our first cop, tied his boat up here.

The next peaked building along (clothes hanging on the line) was George Black's place. Culture came early to town: Black's home held a piano, and his parties were eagerly attended. Black's butcher shop is the next building along. He went into the woods to shoot deer and elk, carved and sold the meat from this building . . . sometimes to boats that were rowed right up to the front door. Our first take-out food spot!

That two-storey building next to Black's is the Granville Hotel, where the elite met. Lord Lansdowne, Canada's Governor General, stayed here on a visit in 1882. This is where the mail came in to be distributed. The fellow who ran the hotel, Joseph Mannion, was called the unofficial "Mayor of Granville." The Moodyville ferry used the Granville Hotel's float.

Then come McKendry's tiny boot and shoe repair shop, run by a fellow whose skill brought him work from as far away as the Cariboo. The squarish white building with the two windows

In 1885, a traveller on the then fast and commodious steamer Maude, from Victoria to Burrard Inlet, would observe on entering the Inlet on his right or south side, a few scattered buildings, along the shore line of the deep bay, then, as now, called Coal Harbor… To reach this place of possibly 150 inhabitants the traveller was obliged to disembark at the wharf at Hastings Mill, about half a mile east of the village, and from there thread his way as best he could along a narrow trail, through dense timber to the only places of public accommodation to be then found on Burrard Inlet… This place in 1872 had been surveyed and platted as a townsite and a few lots…had been sold… But so little was thought of the situation and prospects that only about thirteen lots were bought.

From "Vancouver City", Souvenir Edition, The Vancouver Daily World, 1890

flanking the door was George Brew's restaurant, open when George was not in jail. He tried too often to live up to his surname. Gin Tei Hing's general store (peak top) is next, then Wah Chong's laundry. (Minnie Chong was the first Oriental girl to attend school here. The Hastings Mill School is off the picture to the left, as is the mill itself.)

The big building next in line is Arthur Sullivan's general store. There's a balcony, and we suspect Mr. and Mrs. Sullivan (the town's first Methodist) lived upstairs. Next to them was the dry goods shop of Louis Gold, the town's first Jew. To quote historian Cyril Leonoff, "Gold was a short man, but he reportedly earned the nickname 'Leaping' Louis by springing into the air in the course of some fracas, "swinging his fist mightily and landing with his full weight on his opponent's chin". Such a feat, Leonoff continues, "was enough to win the respect of local loggers, longshoremen and sailors whose attitude toward Jews was not always free of prejudice."

The little white peaked building is the Hole in the Wall Saloon, against which is leaning (!) the doctor's office! Dr. Masters received patients in his little lean-to office. From here on west is a succession of residences. The large building on the right edge of the photo is a boat shed.

There! That tour of the whole business district didn't take long, did it?

There's looming drama in this picture. Two years after it was taken virtually every building and all the trees were destroyed with breathtaking speed by a roaring inferno, and some of the people we've met were consumed in that awful blaze.

Statue of "Gassy Jack" Deighton at sunrise on the old Maple Tree Square at the corner of Water and Carrall, 2001.

"Gassy Jack's" perpetual view of Maple Tree Square as it appeared in 2001.

"A city founded on a public house can't be all bad."
Unknown

"GASSY JACK" DEIGHTON

John Deighton was a talker. A world-class, non-stop, tireless spinner of tales and enthusiastic booster of the prospects of this corner of the Pacific coast. He talked so much, in fact, his customers nicknamed him "Gassy Jack." He was also quick to sense an opportunity, and when he heard of the opening of a new sawmill managed by Edward Stamp on the south shore of Burrard Inlet he acted fast. On the last day of September, 1867 "Gassy Jack" Deighton entered Burrard Inlet with his native wife, her mother, her cousin (who did the rowing), a yellow dog, two chairs and a barrel of whiskey and jovially greeted the men working at Stamp's mill. He knew the nearest drink for these thirsty fellows, and the Moodyville workers across the inlet, was a five-kilometre row east up the inlet to the North Road, then a 12-kilometre walk along that rude trail through the forest, the elk and the bears to New Westminster. He announced to the mill workers they could have all they could drink if they helped him build a bar. The Globe Saloon was up within 24 hours.

John "Gassy Jack" Deighton was a Yorkshireman, born in Hull about 1831. By the late 1850s he was working as a riverboat captain on the Fraser. But he had severe circulatory problems (a contemporary remarked on his complexion of "muddy purple"), and that led to painful swelling of his legs and feet, forcing him to take up another line of work. He opened a bar in New Westminster in 1862, and did well serving drinks to gold seekers on their way to the Cariboo.

When "Gassy Jack" had the sole (saloon) licence he was very dictatorial and would turn out the lights and his customers at 10:30, with a reminder that they had to sleep that they might work for him on the morrow, which they mostly did, as the bulk of their wages used to find their way into Jack's coffers. But when more licences were granted this custom changed, and I have known our mill shut down for a couple of days because so many were engaged in a particularly interesting game that was going on.

From R.H. Alexander, "Reminiscences of the Early Days of B.C.", The Canadian Club of Vancouver: Addresses and Proceedings: 1910-11, 23 February 1911.

View west on Water Street from Carrall, C.1882.

The famous maple tree that gave Gastown's Maple Tree Square its name leans its sheltering leaves over Water Street in this photo, taken around 1882. A protective box helps support it, and shield it from errant carriages. You can almost hear the casual murmur of the conversation among the men sitting on the verandah of John "Gassy Jack" Deighton's hotel. They've seen the photographer and are leaning forward to get a better look.

These fellows on the porch might be discussing the announcement by the Canadian Pacific Railway that they had decided to make Port Moody, at the head of Burrard Inlet, the western terminus of the railway. Surveys were already going on at Port Moody. The CPR's decision to make it Coal Harbour instead is still a few years in the future. Or maybe they're talking about the eerie nighttime glow across the inlet from the electric lights put in at the Moodyville Mill, the first electricity installed north of San Francisco on the Pacific coast.

A few steps west along Water and we see a little boy's rocking horse, a reminder that, yes, there were children here, too. In fact, sharp eyes may see a couple of kids way down at the end of the block. And is that a lamp post down there, ready for the town's one-armed lamplighter John Clough to come along as darkness descends and light it? (Clough was the town's jailer, too, and in charge of the dog pound.)

The telegraph office is the building behind the rocking horse. The telegraph had come to B.C. (New Westminster first) more than 15 years earlier—in fact, the very first message received there over the new device was the news of the assassination April 14, 1865 of U.S. President Abraham Lincoln. (The first telegraph message to leave the province was one sent from New Westminster in April, 1865 to London: "Weather beautiful. All well and Indians perfectly quiet.") Gastown's telegrapher was a bright 21-year-old named Samuel Maclure, who later became an architect and designed many Vancouver buildings, including some of Shaughnessy's finest homes.

The building dimly seen at the far right of the photo is a saloon run by "Portuguese Joe" Silvey.

Again, all that you see here, including the famous maple tree, was destroyed by the Great Fire of June 13, 1886. But from the ashes a brave new city would begin to rise.

Gassy would be thrilled to know this oldest part of Vancouver is called Gastown to this day, more than 130 years after his arrival. His rough-hewn statue (by Vern Simpson), where his first saloon stood, looks out over a neighborhood that is now one of our major tourist attractions. Gassy did very well with his saloon, and built Deighton House in 1870. Two storeys high, it included a hotel, a bar and a billiard parlor. It became so busy that Jack invited his brother Tom to come out from England and work with him. Around the same time, following the death of his first wife, Jack took up with her 12-year-old niece Qua-hail-ya. In 1871 they had a son, Richard. On April 24, 1872 Jack climbed to the top of Deighton House and hoisted atop it the first Canadian flag to fly in Burrard Inlet. (B.C. had joined Confederation the year before). Jack was making renovations to the hotel in anticipation of increased business from the construction of a new road when he fell seriously ill. He died at age 44 on May 29, 1875. His body was taken to New Westminster where it lay in an unmarked grave for 97 years until the Gassy Jack Memorial Fund was established and a headstone erected in 1972.

View south on Carrall from Water Street, 2001.

View south on Carrall from Water Street, 1886. Vancouver Public Library / 001093

A fascinating photograph, and one of Vancouver's most famous. Taken by Harry Devine in early May, 1886, a month after incorporation, it shows the intersection of Water and Carrall Streets. The present-day statue of Gassy Jack is just about where that team of horses is.

The big, bearded man in the centre is George Byrnes, a prominent Victoria auctioneer. The man he's talking to (with his back to us) is local contractor William Brewer, who will years later become the first reeve of South Vancouver.

One of the fellows under the tree (it's unclear which one) is Walter Graveley. Graveley's associated with a colorful early Gastown story: it seems he wanted to move his office building

from "near the waterfront to the corner of Carrall and Cordova Streets." (Cordova is a block south, to the left of the picture.) Telegraph and telephone lines were strung low in those days, and the horse-drawn building jolted one of the poles. As a safety measure, the movers chopped it down! To quote contemporaries, "There was h___ to pay" when that happened. Graveley, incidentally, was the first person to purchase land in Vancouver, buying from the CPR, in 1886, a triangle of property in this very location. He still owned it in 1934.

That poster on the tree is advertising the city's first mayoralty election, just days away. (Only white, male, land-owning residents could vote.)

THE FIRE

It seems hard to believe, but the big picture on this page shows earliest Vancouver before the Great Fire of 1886. Those two men are examining lot boundaries in February, some four months before the June 13 blaze. Vancouver was still a crude jumble of wooden shacks and exposed stumps, fertile ground for a major fire. A CPR crew, burning slash to the west of town on an idle, sunny Sunday, gaped in horror as a freak squall of wind blew in and carried sparks and flames from their small fires into the town. All Vancouver--hundreds and hundreds of buildings, many built between the time of this photograph and the fire--burned to the ground in less than 45 minutes. The death toll has never been definitely established, but was at least eight. The city's hardy pioneers kept their sense of humor, dubbing a crude wooden slapped-together shack with the name of a local (and now vanished) hotel, and setting up City Hall in a big tent (opposite).

TREMONT

Temporary quarters for Tremont Hotel the day after the fire of 1886.
Vancouver Public Library / 009439

Harry Devine took a lot of pictures of early Vancouver. None has been seen more often than this one taken June 16, 1886, a great photograph, a tribute to the gutsy little city that had burned to the ground three days earlier. These are serious men, faced with a serious task, yet posed in an almost comic setting, a tent thrown up in a moment by Alderman Lauchlan Hamilton to provide a backdrop for a group photograph of the city's leaders.

Let's meet these men. Sitting at far left is Ald. Charles A. Coldwell, then comes Ald. E.P. Hamilton and Ald. Joseph R. Northcott. The shorter man looking off to our right (seated under the word "Hall") is our first mayor, Malcolm MacLean. The Scottish born MacLean, 41, a realtor, was a newcomer in town, but since the town itself and many of its inhabitants were also new that didn't count for much. Maclean's only opponent in the May 3rd election was Richard Alexander, the manager of Hastings Sawmill, who had come across as arrogant and grumpy. The election was informal, and marked by questionable practices by both sides. A total of 499 votes was cast, and MacLean won by 17.

Next to MacLean is Ald. Lauchlan Hamilton, the CPR's land commissioner, a man written about elsewhere in this book. Ald. Peter Cordiner is next. The man sitting at the head of the table is Thomas F. McGuigan, the city clerk, whom we learn from Alan Morley's history of Vancouver was at this time courting the daughter of the city's first police chief, John Stewart.

Standing from left: Ald. Joseph Griffith, the one clean-shaven man in this group, Ald. Robert Balfour and then Ald. Thomas Dunn, a hardware merchant. Next is the city solicitor, J.J. Blake. The extravagantly bearded Ald. Joseph Humphries is next, and then city treasurer George F. Baldwin. Standing on the right, the severe Dr. W.J. McGuigan, the coroner. Because of the fire, the death toll of which has been variously estimated at from eight to more than 20 (the fire was so intense there wasn't much left of anything), Dr. McGuigan was a sadly busy man. The empty chair at the left was for Ald. Harry Hemlow, off in Seattle. And that fellow standing on the wharf at left with his hands in his pockets isn't a loafer. He's George W. Gibson, of Gibson's Landing.

The lower picture shows Cordova Street in 1887, the upper in 1890. What a change electricity has brought! The power poles are up in '87, the year electricity was introduced to the city, and by 1890 power is surging through them, lighting stores and homes and streets and powering streetcars. The electricity was generated by a steam plant at the corner of Pender and Abbott Streets.

The streetcar in the upper picture, jammed with passengers celebrating Dominion Day, is #14, the very first electric streetcar to run in Vancouver. In fact, just five days earlier, motorman Aubrey Elliott and conductor Dugald Carmichael had taken #14 out of the "car house" on Barnard Street (now Union Street) and down Westminster Avenue (now Main Street) on a trial run. Two days later, the 9.6-kilometre-system began regular service at five cents a ride. Now, on July 1st, hundreds jam Water Street to cheer the new service and Canada's 23rd birthday.

View to the west along Cordova Street from Carrall, 1887. Vancouver Public Library / 019806

View to the west along Cordova from Carrall, 1890. The year before this picture was taken, the streetcar company had merged with the local illuminating company to create the Vancouver Electric Railway and Light Company Limited. Two corporate descendants: B.C. Hydro and TransLink. Vancouver Public Library / 000974

View west on Water from Carrall, 2001.

View west on Water from Carrall, C.1889. Anchoring this very busy corner is the Alhambra Hotel on the left and the famous Sunnyside Hotel on the right. Just visible behind the Alhambra is the bell tower of Fire Hall #1.
Bailey Brothers / Vancouver Public Library / 013240

View east along Water Street to Carrall, C.1887. Vancouver Public Library / 019806

View westward from the corner of Water and Cordova, 2001.

If it weren't for the flatiron building visible in the lower-right corner of the 1897 photo (right) and the 2001 photo (above), it would be impossible to believe this is the same area. In the century between the two shots the sailing ships have disappeared, as have most of the buildings and CPR rail lines, and new infill areas have been created to add to those already there in 1897. Remember the 1884 photograph that showed the waters of Burrard Inlet lapping right up against Water Street? Today, Water's a long way from water!

One of Gastown's two prominent "flatiron" buildings (the other being the Europe Hotel), is shown under construction in the 1895 photo (right). By 1897 (below) it has blended right in with the waterfront, and the railway trestles, and the sailing ships and the smoke-filled sky. Today, this building–one side on Water, one side on Cordova–houses a variety of retail shops.

F.R.STEWART & CO

KELLY DOUGLAS CO

HUDSON'S BAY COMPANY.

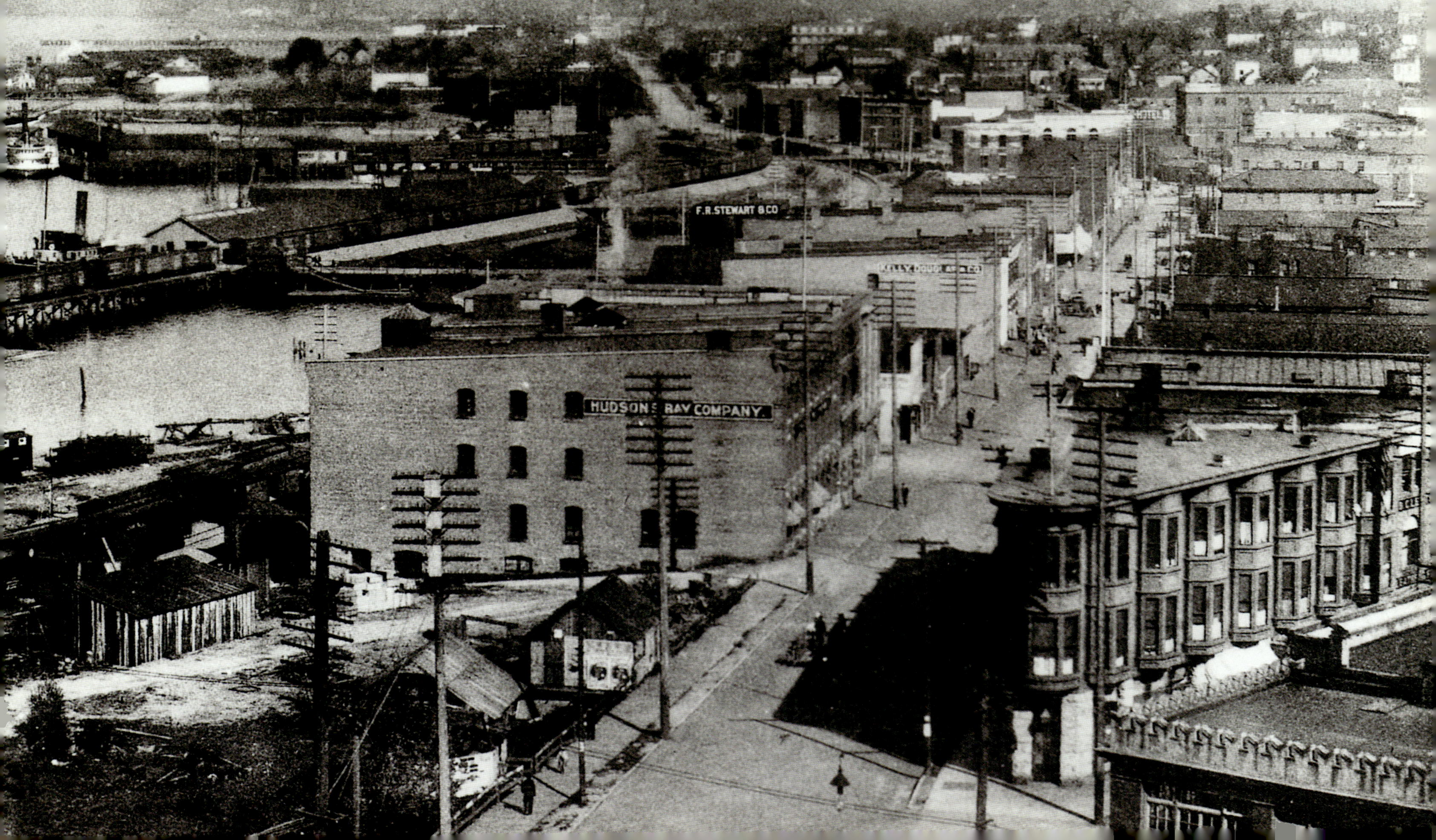

FIRE DEPARTMENT

Hose wagon attending to fire, C.1895 Vancouver Public Library / 005486

Firefighters working at the corner of Manitoba and 2nd Avenue West as kids watch the unfolding drama from the relative safety of a tall fence, C.1919.
Vancouver Public Library / 006648

Fire on CPR Pier 'D' at the foot of Granville, 1938. Vancouver Public Library / 006365

The Vancouver Fire Department had a terribly dramatic beginning. Mere weeks after the city was incorporated (April 6, 1886) practically the entire city was destroyed in the Great Fire of June 13, 1886. The little volunteer department had no equipment to fight a blaze of this extent, and could only watch helplessly as hundreds of buildings were consumed by flame. The city's firefighting tools, department historian Alex Matches has written, "consisted of the city's axes, buckets, shovels and ladders and little else." A few days after the fire, city council agreed to the purchase of a horse-drawn Ronald fire engine, manufactured in Brussels, Ontario.

The first major fire fought by the department, using the Ronald, was at Spratt's Oilery. The oilery, department records indicate, was "at a considerable distance from town." Today, we know the location as the north foot of Burrard Street, about where the Marine Building is. Unfortunately, the little department had no horses, so they had to physically drag the engine to the fire along the city's rough streets. They weren't able to save the oilery, but they did prevent nearby houses from burning and were properly lauded for their valiant efforts.

Things are very different today: the VFD now has computer-equipped apparatus (feeding them vital information on the blaze as they roar along to get to it), there are female firefighters, and training in handling hazardous material spills and in the use of defibrillators to aid heart-attack victims. Special training in confined-space and high-angle rescue is now in place. There's even a division that handles stunt requests from movie makers: special stunts, especially those involving fire, now need advance approval.

Firefighters pose with their gleaming hose wagon, C.1890.
Vancouver Public Library / 006365

Group of visiting fire chiefs pose with the firefighters of Fire Hall No. 6 on Nicola Street in the West End, 1908.
Vancouver Public Library / 019788

Vancouver's first fire chief was a remarkable man named John Howe Carlisle. Determined that a great fire, like the one in 1886, would never happen again he persuaded council to install automatic call boxes on major corners, making Vancouver the first city on the continent to do so. In 1907 he purchased three motorized fire engines, making the city one of the earliest in North America to bid farewell to the horse-and buggy era. Under Carlisle's inspired leadership, Vancouver's young department was ranked third in the world (after London and Leipzig) by a committee of international experts. The city rewarded this far-seeing man by keeping him as chief for an astonishing 42 years, from 1886 to 1928.

Firefighters of Fire Hall No. 6 posing in front of their remodeled station on Nicola Street, 2001.

CITY HALL

Vancouver Police Department posing in front of make-shift City Hall on June 14th, 1886, the day after the great fire.
Harry Devine / Vancouver Public Library / 001090

Constable Charles Parks on bike patrol in Stanley Park, C.1900.
Vancouver Police Centennial Museum

Constables Cal Traversy and Tony Chambers talking with a couple visiting from Pearland, Texas, 2001.

After the first council meeting civic organization was, more or less, complete, but there was no money in the treasury, and the question of finances came up early… Some money was collected from fines inflicted on disorderly or drunken persons, but they were very small amounts, two dollars and fifty cents, went to pay the police salaries.

W.H. Gallagher, quoted in J.S. Matthews,
Early Vancouver, volume 1, number Page 1

POLICE DEPARTMENT

The four-man police department that maintained the law in 1886 Vancouver (upper left) was four times as big as the force that had performed the same role in Gastown. Jonathan Miller was our first constable (ununiformed), and his duties also allowed him time to be the tax collector. The Gaoler's Mews police station where he made his home was a tiny government-built log cottage facing Cordova Street. There were two small cells for miscreants, but they had no locks. When you were sentenced to a term in them, you were considered honor bound to stay there. When Vancouver was created, Miller became the first postmaster and a formal police department (uniformed) was formed, with John Stewart as chief. That's Stewart under the word "city" in that famous photo. Their badges were made from American silver dollars, with one side smoothed down and engraved Vancouver City Police, and the other with a pin soldered on.

As the city grew, so did the force. By 1912 they had a chief's car, a detective car, a paddy wagon and an ambulance. They also had two women members, although Nancy Harris and Minnie Miller were confined to administrative duties. They'd acquired a patrol car by the early 1920s, a Hudson Speedster that had been stolen in Los Angeles and recovered here. The American insurance company that claimed it sold it to the city rather than have the car driven all the way back over the gravel roads of the day.

Constable Duncan McTavish utilizing high-tech traffic signal to keep things moving at the corner of Hastings and Abbott, C.1920. Vancouver Police Centennial Museum

Group portrait of a much expanded Vancouver Police Department, 1903. The elderly, one-armed officer seated at right is the famous John Clough, Vancouver's original jailer and lamplighter back in 1886. He was also the first person to draw a pension from the city.
Vancouver Police Centennial Museum

Today, there are more than 1,100 members of the Vancouver Police Department. The force's official web site lists 101 different areas: Arson Squad, Bicycle Squad (with more than 60 members on bikes), Mounted Squad, the Drug Unit, Burglary Squad, School Liaison Team, Business Liaison Unit and dozens more, including the Odd Squad, a society comprised of police officers "dedicated to educating the public on issues affecting the community." There are well over 100 women on the force, in almost all ranks. Traffic, one of the department's primary concerns, has grown and intensified hugely since 1920's Constable McTavish (above) was able to control the flow at a busy city intersection with a hand-held sign.

And, in a development that would astonish Chief Stewart, the department has now introduced Internet Citizen Reporting. Reports of property crime offences where there is no suspect may now be reported through the Internet. Property crime offences include Theft (including Theft From Autos) and Mischief (Damage to Property or Vandalism).

On an informal note, the award-winning Vancouver Police Pipe Band is hugely popular, and is asked to perform at many functions throughout the year.

Officer on foot patrol along Granville, 1907.
Vancouver Public Library / 001090

HUDSON'S BAY COMPANY

Hudson's Bay Company's first store on Cordova Street, C1888. It would appear that the company knew the value of home delivery early on. Leonard Frank / Vancouver Public Library / 006354

Hudson's Bay Company's first store on the corner of Granville and Georgia between 1895 and 1900.
Vancouver Public Library / 007990

Vancouver was just a couple of years old when this photograph (left, above) was taken on Cordova. But the Hudson's Bay Co., which opened here January 17, 1887, had been active in the rest of Canada for more than 200 years and knew a thing or two about running a store. Their three-storey location in Winnipeg, for example, had opened in 1881 and–because Winnipeg was a sizable town–offered an astonishing range of goods, including Russian caviar, silk lingerie and musical instruments. The range of goods wasn't quite as wide yet in this first, small Vancouver location–photographer Leonard Frank has managed to get the entire staff into one shot–and the store held only what it called the "necessities of life." That meant saws, axes, lanterns and provisions.

The manager, George Weeks, lived in rooms at the back of the store. But this was no one-horse operation: there were two horses.

There was something you could buy at Hudson's Bay stores then that you can't now: wine and spirits. Trade in booze was brisk enough that when the store opened a second location on Granville Street north of Georgia in 1890, the Cordova Street location was retained just to warehouse and sell it. It closed in 1893 when a new store was built at the northeast corner of Granville and Georgia, the Bay's present location. It's the homely three-storey red brick building to the right of the streetcar in the photo at lower left. It opened September 21, 1893. This was the "happening" part of town: kitty-corner from the store was the Hotel Vancouver, and the CPR's lavish Vancouver Opera House was just a few steps away.

Competition in the dry goods trade in Vancouver was brisk. One particularly successful shop had been opened in 1892 on Westminster Avenue (now Main Street) just south of Hastings by a man named Charles Woodward.

The horse is still king of the Hudson's Bay Company's delivery fleet but the few trucks at the end of the line signal the beginning of the end, C.1917. National Archives of Canada / PA 122056

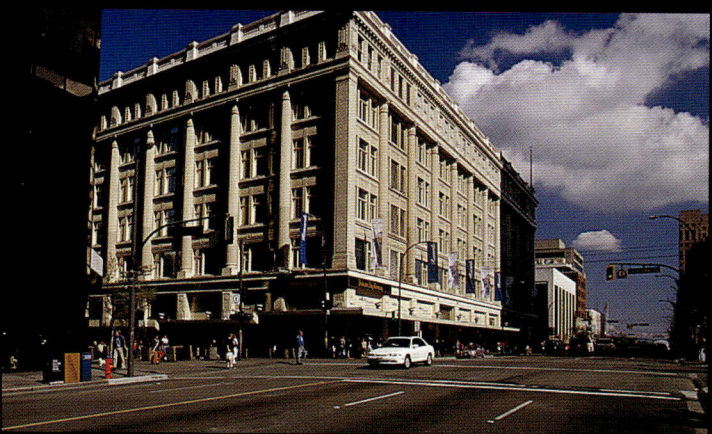

The Bay, at the corner of Georgia and Granville, 2001.

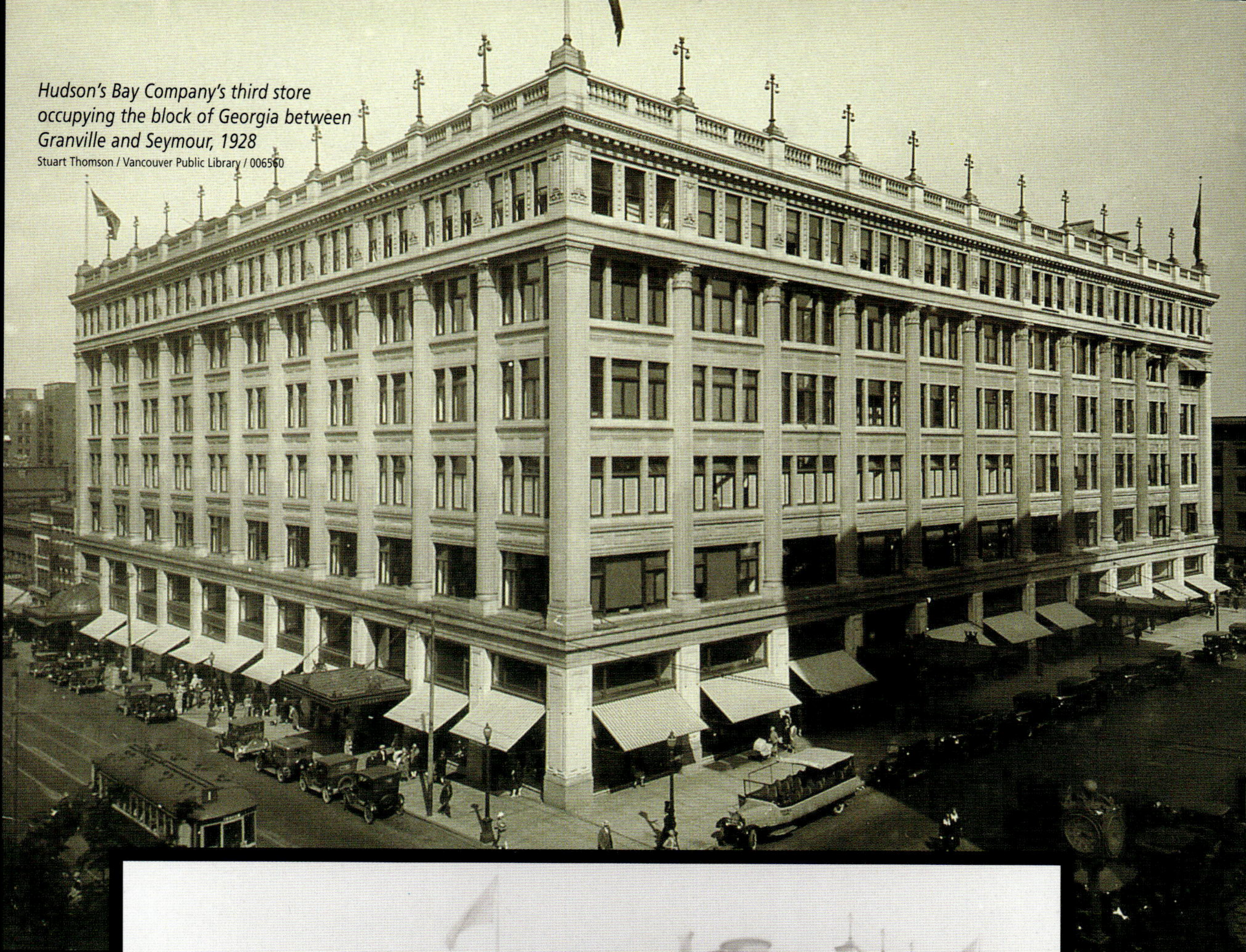

Hudson's Bay Company's third store occupying the block of Georgia between Granville and Seymour, 1928
Stuart Thomson / Vancouver Public Library / 006560

If you'd been able to pull up a chair at the corner of Granville and Georgia in 1893 and sit there for 33 years watching the northeast corner, you'd have seen a number of changes to the Bay. Six years into your vigil, 1899, you'd see the store extended by 50 feet north along Granville. Then, in 1905, a 25-foot extension stretched the store east along Georgia. (You can see that latter extension in the photo at bottom right, snuggled up against the taller, white building at back.)

But they were just getting started: in 1913, construction began at Georgia and Seymour on the first phase of the present store, right behind the old store on Granville. This new space is that aforementioned taller, white building. That addition opened to shoppers March 14, 1914. In 1925 (how's that chair holding out?) the old three-storey store at Granville and Georgia was torn down and replaced with the present one, joined to the 1914 building and continuing its cream terra cotta facing and Corinthian columns. Next, in 1926, more store was added to the north on Granville Street. The 1928 photo at upper right shows that. You can take your chair and leave now: you won't be able to see the 1949 Seymour Street addition from your perch.

When you step into the Bay today you're entering a Vancouver store that has had, literally, nine lives.

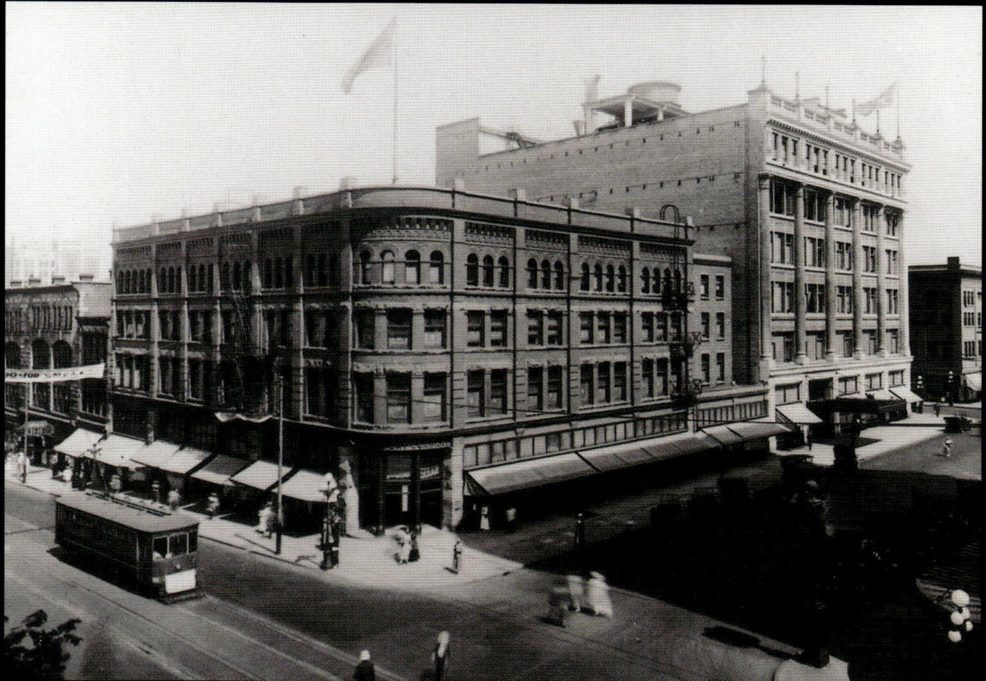

Here we see the two stores operating at the same time, C.1917 It is interesting to watch the growth of the two stores on Georgia through the first 30 years of the 20th century. Is that the Birks Building (1913-94) casting its shadow on both stores, the old and the new? National Archives of Canada / PA-122004

Vancouver Public Library / 025644

SHOPPING

This (left) is what grocery shopping looked like 60 years ago. Truth to tell, it doesn't seem all that different! All the women are wearing hats, it's true, and there are no men in sight… but aside from the old-fashioned lighting, and what seems an inordinate variety of canned peas, Woodward's of 1941 looks fairly familiar. Dollars to donuts that shopping cart even has a wobbly wheel! Twenty years later (lower left), still at Woodward's, and the basic idea is still evident, but now there's brighter lighting, a few men have shown up and there's a section called Specialty Foods. More exotic fare is beginning to show up on grocery shelves.

Vancouver Public Library / 077977E

Save-On-Foods in White Rock, 2001.

City of Vancouver Archives / BU 675 N558

Today's health inspectors would blanch at this spectacle, with all that unrefrigerated meat hanging around. (Often, the back and front doors were left open so that air would circulate in the shops.) We liked our meat in the 1890s, and is it possible this is one of the butcher shops all in a row that gave Gastown's Blood Alley its name? As Vancouver grew, its residents began to demand not only high quality beef but also that beef be available all year round. That made the interior ranching industry viable. But beef wasn't all there was: Vancouver's early butchers often bought wild game and fowl (deer, elk, grouse) from professional hunters, who went out into the surrounding forest to make a living. One such marksman, a Prussian named Alvo von Alvensleben, came to Vancouver with pennies in his pocket and parlayed his shooting skill (and a gift of the gab) into enough income to make a modest entry into the real estate market. He ended up one of Vancouver's first millionaires.

Shop at 605 West Hastings advertising the fact that it catered to gold seekers headed to find their mother lode in the Klondike. Vancouver Public Library / 009493

Zebulon Franks Hardware shop at 42 Water Street, 1887. City of Vancouver Archives / BU P557 N731#5

It was rough, but it was ready. This (left) is one of the more famous of Vancouver's early shops, Zebulon Franks' Hardware store at 42 Water Street. It's 1887, and the town is still rebuilding itself after the Great Fire of June 13, 1886. Business is good. Zebulon Franks himself was an interesting man. The son of a rabbi, he had escaped from a pogrom near Odessa in the Ukraine to become the first lay religious leader of Vancouver's Jewish community. Later, he would be instrumental in the construction of the city's first synagogue.

It was the Klondike Gold Rush of the late 1800s and early 1900s that brought Vancouver its first boom. Shops ready to outfit the gold seekers popped up all along the coast, in Portland, Seattle, Victoria and Vancouver. Page Ponsford Brothers at 605 West Hastings (above, about 1900) did a roaring business… appropriately enough, the Vancouver Board of Trade had its offices directly above. (The first banquet of our Board of Trade, by the way, was held March 5, 1889 in the Hotel Vancouver, at a cost of $12.50 per plate. That was expensive for the time, but then it included a quart bottle of Mumm's Extra Dry Champagne.) One staffer at Page Ponsford was a young fellow named Edward Chapman, who went on to establish his own famous clothing shops. We don't think the store provided the oxen.

The Klondike rush appealed to hardened, professional prospectors roving the world's gold fields. For them it was an opportunity to return to the days before industrial mining took hold, a last chance for adventure and riches, even if it was fleeting. "Nothing will come of him," one of these men wrote about himself and his fellow prospectors. "He is a word in the wind, a brother to the fog. At the scene of his activity no memory of him will remain."

Well stocked interior of Dawson's Hardware at 65 East Hastings, C.1908 Philip Timms / Vancouver Public Library / 005381

Dawson's Hardware, at 65 East Hastings Street, was the Home Depot of its day. Everything you could want for maintenance and repairs to the home of 1908 was there. Did you need sheets of fancy embossed tin for your dining room ceiling? A new kerosene lamp? A bucket to carry the gasoline for your automobile? Nails for your horse's shoes? A wood stove? LaVal cream separator? Bissell's new carpet sweeper? Saw nuts, porcelain sconces, birdcages, neatsfoot oil… anything you needed!

Interior and exterior views of The Home Depot in Burnaby, 2001.

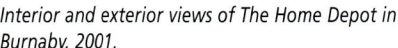

"THE PIONEER GAS STATION OF CANADA"

was opened in 1908 at the corner of Cambie and Smithe.
John Innes City of Vancouver Archives / Trans P3 N3

Sometime around 1907 it occurred to the Vancouver office of the Imperial Oil Co. that the usual method of fueling automobiles–carrying a sloshing bucket full of gasoline up to the vehicle and pouring it through a funnel into the tank–was somewhat dangerous. The manager of Imperial's Vancouver office, Charles Rolston, was also concerned that a number of local garages were overcharging for the gas. He felt that reflected badly on Imperial, at the time the sole source of the fuel.

So, adjacent to the company's storage yard and facing the street he built a small open- sided shed of corrugated iron. Atop a tapering concrete pillar he placed a 13-gallon kitchen water tank "fitted with a glass steam-gauge marked off by white dots in one-gallon increments." The tank was gravity fed, being connected to Imperial's main storage tank. The filling hose was a ten- foot length of garden hose, drained with thumb and finger by the attendant after filling a car. The first attendant was Imperial's former night watchman, J.C. Rollston (no relation to Charles Rolston), who had been in poor health. His coworkers believed he would improve in the sun and open air. They bought a barroom chair for him and set him down.

Canada's first "gas station" was now in business. That's a painting of it (left) by John Innes. Soon all of the cars in Vancouver were purchasing their gas at the Smithe and Cambie Street station (southeast corner). A mini biography of Rolston says that on pre-holiday afternoons there were as many as 50 to 60 automobiles lined up waiting to be fueled. He added a second tank.

It's sometimes claimed that this was the world's first gas station. Not by a long shot. A detailed history of an 1898 operation in Cedar Rapids, Iowa makes it clear where that honor lies. But this was certainly Canada's first.

ESSO service station in North Vancouver, 2001.

The city council at its special meeting yesterday afternoon, discussed the increasing number of automobile accidents, the advisability of framing some regulation requiring new drivers of cars to qualify for competency before being allowed to drive on business streets, and the damage done to pavements by heavy trucks, and finally appointed a special committee to enquire into the whole question.

It is 1928, just 20 years since C.M. Rolston, opened the country's first gas station and nary a horse in sight. Here we see a thriving Blackburns Garage at 822 Seymour (corner of Robson). Sales, repair, storage and even what might be Vancouver's first car-wash. Mr. Blackburn certainly seems to be a fan of Henry Ford...

Petro-Canada service station in North Vancouver, 2001

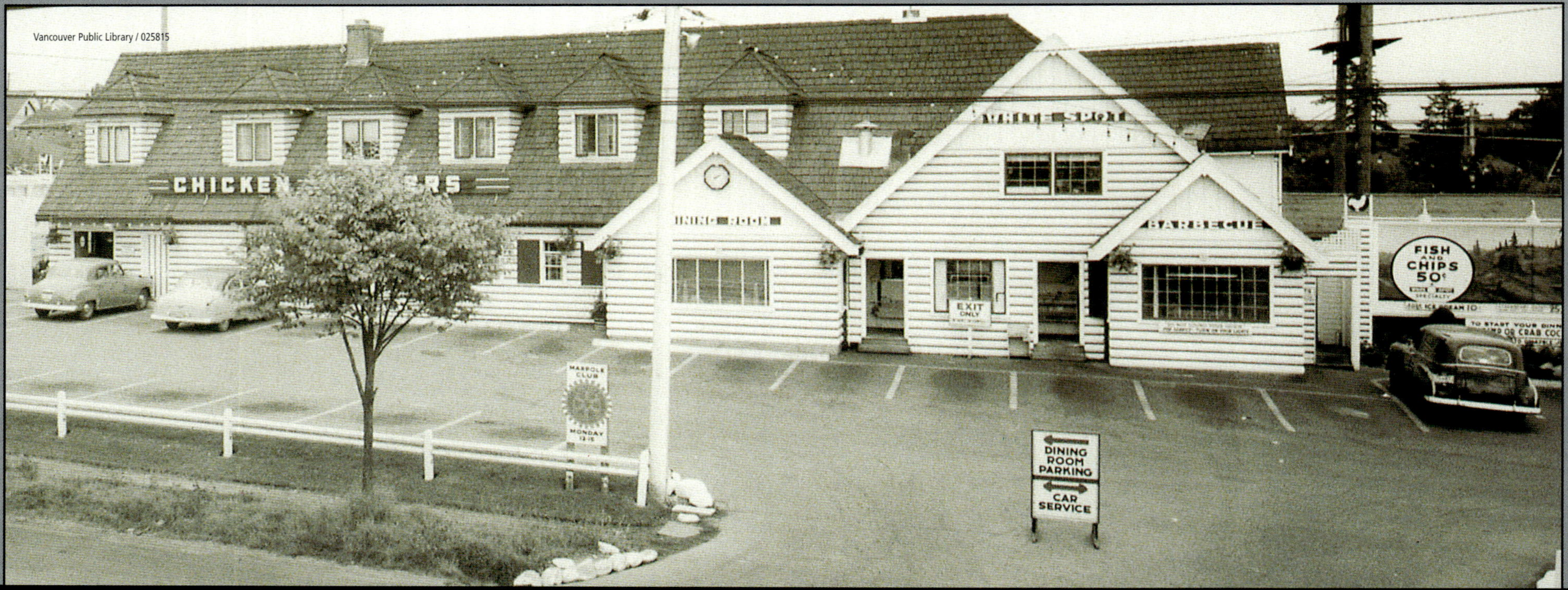

Vancouver Public Library / 025815

Vancouver Public Library / 009001

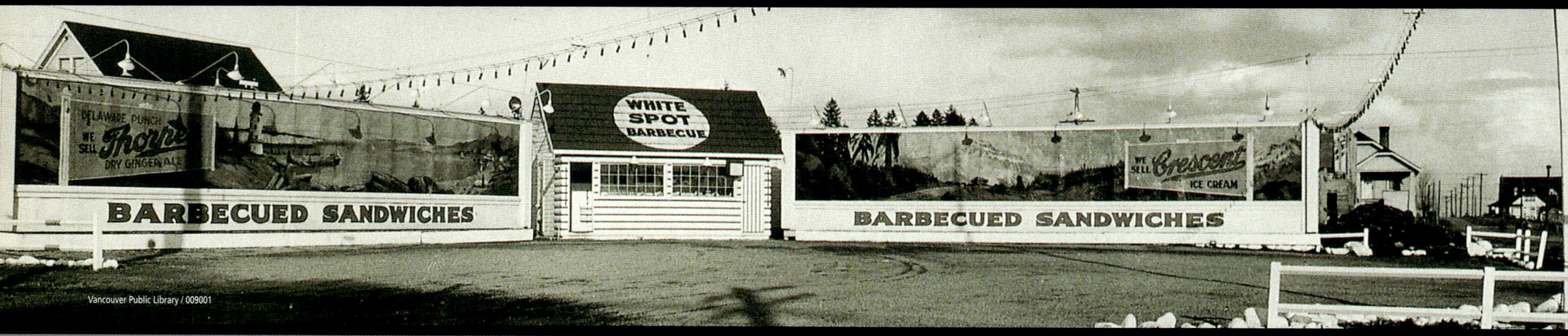

The car changed just about everything, including the way we ate. A young fellow named Nat Bailey caught on to that quickly. He had a 1918 Model T truck, and converted it into a travelling lunch counter, parking every Sunday at Lookout Point on SW Marine Drive. Hungry sightseers crowded around, paid a dime for a hot dog, a nickel for an ice cream. On one hot summer day in 1924, a customer leaned out his car and shouted, "Why don't you bring it to us?" That was the inspiration. Four years later, in June of 1928, Nat Bailey, then just 26, proudly welcomed guests to the first White Spot drive-in on Granville at 67th (small photo), and the legend began.

Even in 1952 (large photo) a fish-and-chips or chicken dinner at the White Spot cost just 50 cents.

If there was anything happening in Vancouver in the 1940s and beyond, CKNW deejay Jack Cullen (right, in 1948) would be there. The car was a gift from heaven for the irrepressible Cullen, who did his whole radio show from a Black Top cab one night, popping in to the White Spot for a quick on-air snack. Cullen did his Owl Prowl show from rooftops, from listeners' homes, did one show naked at the YMCA pool . . . he was everywhere, and everyone listened. Vancouver Public Library / 080643

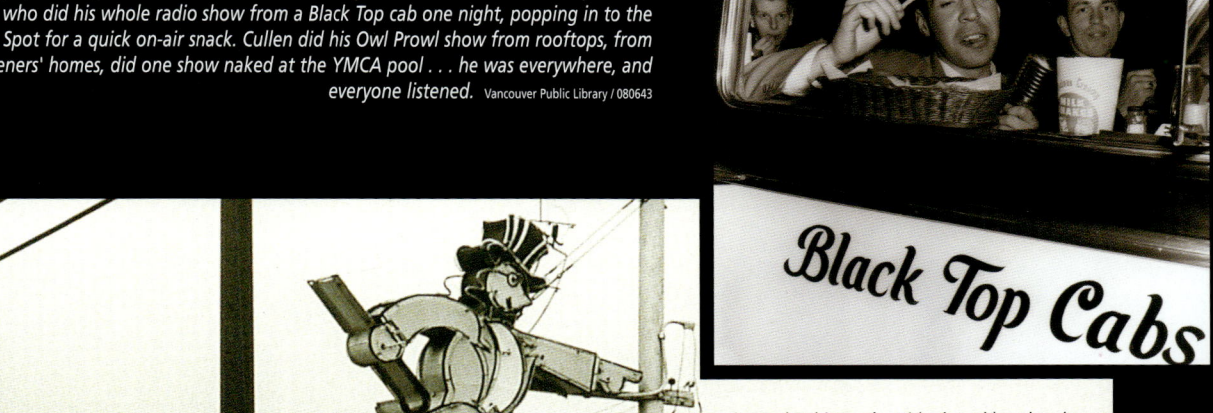

Deejay Red Robinson (outside the cab) and author Chuck Davis (inside) digging Gastown, 2001.

DINE IN YOUR CAR

Yes, people were eating in their cars more than 50 years ago. From the White Spot here at 13th and Granville (in 1951), you might cruise the streets for a while just digging the scene, then bop over to the drive-in theatre to see The Day the Earth Stood Still, then tool out to Point Grey with your favorite girl to "watch the submarine races". The impact of the automobile on cities like Vancouver is beyond calculation.

And when Elvis Presley burst onto the mid-50s music scene, Vancouver deejay Red Robinson was there to catch the wave . . . and, before anyone else in town was doing it, to air stars like Fats Domino, Roy Orbison, Little Richard and Buddy Holly. And where did most kids listen? In their cars! Red was a giant in Vancouver radio for more than 40 years, changed the listening habits of a generation.

This was New Brighton, the "End of the Road." (Douglas Road, only portions of which exist today.) The gentleman in the foreground admiring the horse and its mount in this 1886 photo is the ever-active George Black, owner of the Hastings Hotel, the two-storey building in the background. The hotel was built as the New Brighton in 1865 by Oliver Hocking as a summer resort for people from New Westminster. The pleasure-seekers got to the hotel, at the north foot of what is now Windermere Street, on a stagecoach that ran a regular Douglas Road service from New Westminster. The coach's arrival was announced with three blood-stirring blasts from a bugle. Could that horse and open carriage in the background of this photo be part of the hotel's not-so-rapid transit service?

In 1866 hotelier Hocking became Deputy Collector of Customs at Burrard Inlet. That meant captains of ships docking in the inlet (including Moodyville, on the north shore) no longer had to walk the more than a dozen kilometres through the woods—where encounters with bears were not uncommon–to New Westminster to get their papers. (This hotel was also the docking spot for various Burrard Inlet ferry systems over the years.) In 1869 a remarkable fellow named Maximilien Michaud, who had walked to the Pacific coast from Quebec, bought the New Brighton from Hocking and renamed it the Hastings Hotel. Maxie Michaud became the unofficial postmaster: you could pop into his hotel and pick up your mail from a shelf in the kitchen. Michaud eventually sold the hotel to George Black.

The dashing George Black was a gambler and an entrepreneur. As a sideline, he arranged horse races down Granville Street in early Vancouver. This is likely one of his thoroughbreds, with a young boy pressed into service as a jockey.

BRIGHTON

Where tiny Brighton once meandered its slow days away at the end of a rough and ready road from New Westminster, there has been an astonishing transformation a century later: the massive grain elevators of Cascadia Terminal (formerly the Alberta Wheat Pool) loom over the waters of the Second Narrows; a waiting ship takes on grain; an army of boxcars crowds against the elevators; an unending stream of cars and trucks and vacationers' RVs rumbles over the Ironworkers Memorial Second Narrows Bridge; the CNR's railway bridge spans the inlet (and crosses over the CPR line on the south shore); while across the inlet the north shore hums with industrial activity... this is one of the most transformed spots in the entire Lower Mainland.

Stand in this spot with the traffic roaring past, and it's virtually impossible to close your eyes and transport yourself in your imagination back to the days when it was so quiet you could shout across the inlet for Navvy Jack to row over and pick you up.

Even when more advanced ferries began their service, their quiet chugging added very little to the local soundscape... although one particularly rustic craft was nicknamed the "Sudden Jerk" for its tendency to vigorously shake up passengers and cargo as it got underway. In addition, the boat's engine was chained to the deck. The engine had once fallen through the deck and into the saltchuck, and the chain was attached to prevent a reoccurrence.

Today, Vancouver's the biggest port in Canada, (bigger than the next three combined) biggest on the west coast of North America, and the biggest on the continent in tonnage of foreign exports, an economic powerhouse that contributes more than $1 billion to the local economy every year, directly employs 11,000 people, and ships people and goods to more than 100 countries around the world. Now that's transformation!

Aerial view eastwards over Brighton Park to 2nd Narrows Bridge and Burnaby Heights, 2001.

View from downtown over Centennial Pier and Burrard Inlet to 2nd narrows Bridge, 2001. The CPR right of way can be seen snaking its way along the shore of the inlet on the same roadbed that opened the area to expansion in 1887.

81

View to the west along Hastings from Homer, 1909. Philip Timms / Vancouver Public Library / 005229

View to the east along Hastings from Homer, 1909.
Philip Timms / Vancouver Public Library / 005221

HASTINGS

Vancouver was in the middle of an astonishing building boom in 1909 when Philip Timms took these pictures (facing page) of West Hastings Street. Looking west from Homer (top) you can see the clock-topped tower of the Post Office (now part of Sinclair Centre) at the corner of Granville, under construction when this picture was taken. The clock hasn't been installed yet. Tucked away along this stretch are a couple of other notable buildings still with us: the Winch Building–just behind the Post Office at 757 West Hastings and also now part of Sinclair Centre -and the Bank of Commerce at 640-698 West Hastings, a handsome structure occupied today by Birks Jewelers. Several less architecturally distinguished buildings survive, an echo of a time when the downtown pace was slower, when a big store could sell all sorts of stuff for 15 cents or less (see the sign above the streetcar in the lower picture), and when traffic ran the opposite way.

The building under construction in the lower picture is the Dominion Trust Building, at Cambie and Hastings, one of the most recognizable structures in the city and, for a brief time, the tallest building in the British Empire… at just 147 feet, 6 inches! It's not even among the city's 35 highest buildings today. It was called "the most modern office building in Canada," and, says Bruce Macdonald in Vancouver: A Visual History, "helped make investment money available for use in Vancouver."

That money was attracted to the city because of its astonishing growth, from 27,010 people in the 1901 census to 100,401 in 1911!

View to the west along Hastings from Homer, 2001.

View to the east along Hastings from Seymour, 2001.

Looking like something from an Italian painting, this was Vancouver's original courthouse as it appeared C.1905. Built in 1888, it quickly proved too small and was demolished in 1912 when the larger courthouse was opened on Georgia Street. Where this building stood is now the site of the Cenotaph at Victory Square. City of Vancouver Archives / BU P420 N404

VICTORY SQUARE

Because of its location and its triangular shape, Victory Square has been called the "keystone" of Vancouver. The Province newspaper, (across Cambie Street in the Carter-Cotton Building, still there at 198 West Hastings), contributed funds for the transformation of the former courthouse site into a park memorial to the fallen of World War One. The public helped financially, too. When the park was dedicated in April, 1924 it was named Victory Square. More than 25,000 people, many of them veterans, jammed the streets at the opening ceremony.

The Cenotaph is a grey obelisk, 30 feet high, made of Nelson Island granite—and three sided to conform to the shape of the park. Its flags are changed regularly.

Today, this intersection marks the western edge of the Downtown Eastside, an economically depressed area that in the early years of the 21st century is making a slow and difficult ascent to better times.

Look at the building behind the Cenotaph in the photograph opposite. (There's a sign for Jacoby Bros. on the facade.) The near corner of that building is the southwest corner of Hamilton and Hastings Streets, and the reason that's important is that it was at that very spot in 1885 that CPR land commissioner Lauchlan Hamilton stood, in the middle of a forest, and commenced to lay out and name the streets of what we now know as downtown Vancouver: Pender, Granville, Georgia and so on. And the very first street name Hamilton bestowed? Hamilton!

View west along Hastings from Cambie to Burrard, 2001. Two of Vancouver's finest, the Dominion Building in the right foreground and the Marine Building, marking the spot in the distance where Hastings takes a little jog to the left after crossing Burrard, stand proudly as architectural monuments of an earlier age.

It's 1936, and Vancouver has turned 50. With the amalgamation of South Vancouver and Point Grey in 1929, we have a population of about 260,000. The Depression is battering the country, and Vancouver is not spared, but we put on a brave face and celebrate the birthday with parades and special events. The Dominion Building (right) looks splendid.
Vancouver Public Library / 006439

The corner of Cambie and Hastings, looking west along Hastings, in 1904. The building at the left edge of the photograph, at Hamilton and Hastings, is still there in 1936 (below), but minus its tower! Vancouver Public Library / 005292

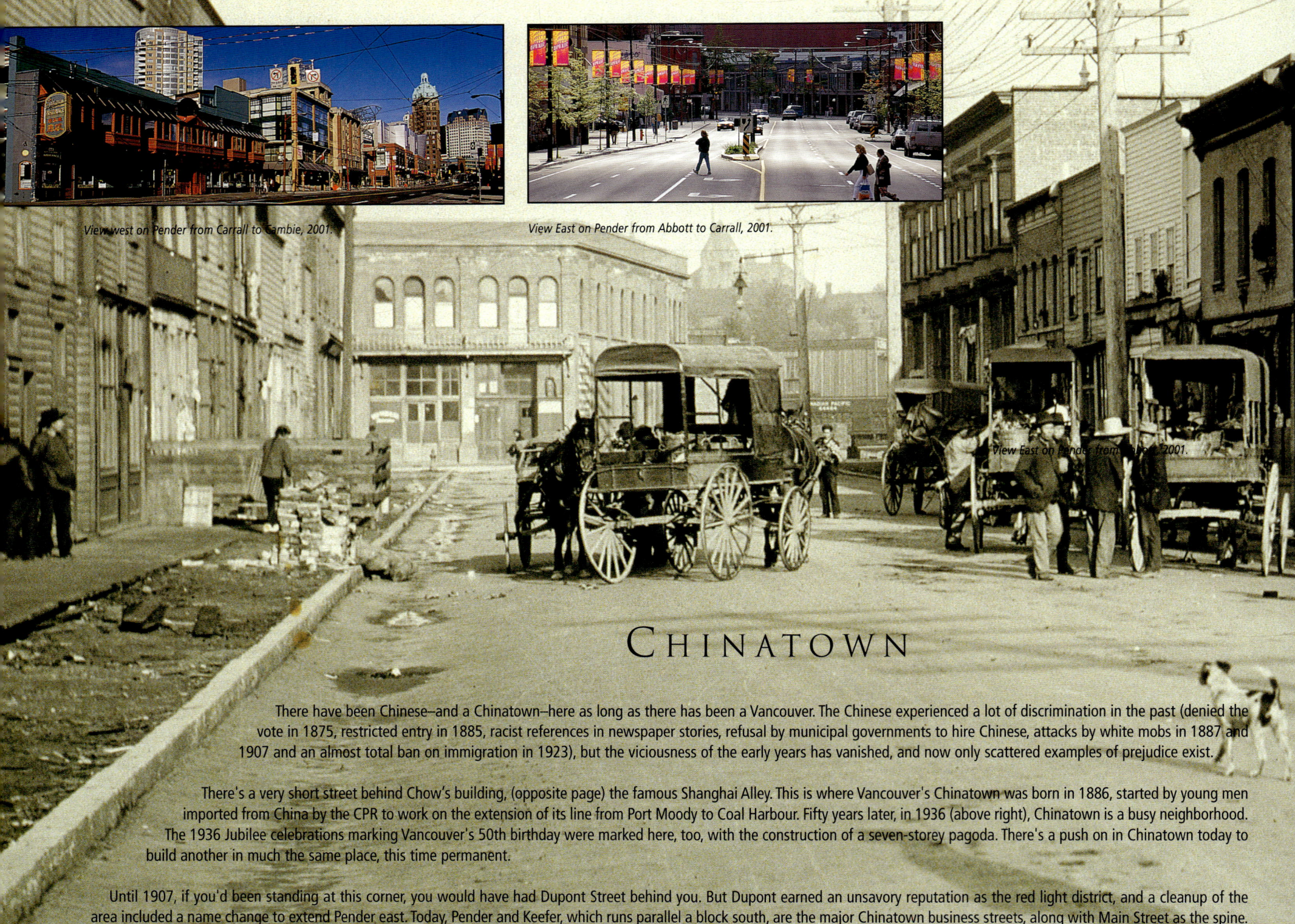

View west on Pender from Carrall to Cambie, 2001.

View East on Pender from Abbott to Carrall, 2001.

View East on Pender from Abbott, 2001.

CHINATOWN

There have been Chinese—and a Chinatown—here as long as there has been a Vancouver. The Chinese experienced a lot of discrimination in the past (denied the vote in 1875, restricted entry in 1885, racist references in newspaper stories, refusal by municipal governments to hire Chinese, attacks by white mobs in 1887 and 1907 and an almost total ban on immigration in 1923), but the viciousness of the early years has vanished, and now only scattered examples of prejudice exist.

There's a very short street behind Chow's building, (opposite page) the famous Shanghai Alley. This is where Vancouver's Chinatown was born in 1886, started by young men imported from China by the CPR to work on the extension of its line from Port Moody to Coal Harbour. Fifty years later, in 1936 (above right), Chinatown is a busy neighborhood. The 1936 Jubilee celebrations marking Vancouver's 50th birthday were marked here, too, with the construction of a seven-storey pagoda. There's a push on in Chinatown today to build another in much the same place, this time permanent.

Until 1907, if you'd been standing at this corner, you would have had Dupont Street behind you. But Dupont earned an unsavory reputation as the red light district, and a cleanup of the area included a name change to extend Pender east. Today, Pender and Keefer, which runs parallel a block south, are the major Chinatown business streets, along with Main Street as the spine. The recent explosive growth of the Chinese community in Richmond has slowed the pace in Vancouver's Chinatown somewhat, but it is still an exciting and colorful place to shop, sightsee and eat.

View west on Pender to Carrall, 1904. Philip Timms / Vancouver Public Library / 007234

View west on Pender from Main, 2001.

The Sam Kee Building (below), erected in 1912, is one of the most well-known buildings in the city. The owner, Chang Toy (Sam Kee was not a person, but the name of Chang's company), had a portion of his property at the southwest corner of Carrall and Pender Streets expropriated by the city, which was widening Pender. Chang was compensated for the expropriation, and he was also left a six-foot-wide strip of land, unneeded by the city. The owner of the adjacent building offered to buy the little strip, but Chang decided to put a building up on it! Just six feet wide, it's claimed to be the narrowest building in the world. An argument has been made that a house at Singel 7 in Amsterdam, at just one metre wide, takes the skinny prize. But only the front façade of the Amsterdam house is really so narrow; behind that it broadens out to normal proportions. (Jack Chow, the owner of the Sam Kee Building today, says he's the winner.)

Sam Kee building in 2001 and 1936 City of Vancouver Archives / BU P253 N158#1

Dr. Sun Yat-Sen Classical Garden

The Dr. Sun Yat-Sen Garden is the first full-scale classical garden ever constructed outside China. It is modeled after private classical gardens developed in the City of Suzhou during the Ming Dynasty (1368–1644).

Financing and construction represent a unique cooperative effort between Canada and the People's Republic of China. A 52–member team of experts from the City of Suzhou spent an entire year constructing the Garden. Working with them were Vancouver architect Joe Wai and landscape architect Don Vaughan.

Opened in the Spring of 1986 in time for Expo 86, the Garden was named in honour of the memory of Dr. Sun Yat-Sen, the Father of modern China. Dr. Sun played a leading role in the overthrow of the oppressive Ching Dynasty in 1911 and was the first president of the Republic of China.

Water Pavilion and Corridor Pavilion viewed from the adjacent Dr. Sun Yat-Sen Park and the Chinese Cultural Centre. The Garden is designed to incorporate "borrowed" views from the adjoining park.

View west on Hastings from Hamilton, C.1905
Vancouver Public Library / 006678

There's one thing we know for certain about the early years of the 20th century: the hat business was booming. Everyone, men, women and children, wore hats. Note, in this Hastings Street scene (about 1905), the elegant couple being shaded by the lady's frilly little parasol.

To the right, a splendid 1931 Stuart Thomson view of Pender Street west from Cambie. Students at the City Centre Campus of Vancouver Community College might enjoy seeing what the neighborhood looked like more than 70 years ago. But where's the traffic?

View to the west along Pender from Cambie, C.1939 Stuart Thomson / Vancouver Public Library / 006559

View to the west along Pender from Cambie, 2001. The building visible at bottom right in both pictures is now home to the Architectural Institute of British Columbia.

View to the north west over the corner of Georgia and Cambie, 2000.

North west corner of Georgia and Cambie, 1936. Vancouver Public Library / 007876 and 007875

Yes, the rows of houses in those 1936 photos are on the same stretch of Cambie and Georgia Streets as the Queen Elizabeth Theatre is today. That peaked building at the far end of the Georgia Street picture (left) is Holy Rosary Cathedral. At the far end of the Cambie Street picture (right) is the Carter-Cotton Building, home then of the Province newspaper. A trend toward broad, open plazas began in Vancouver in the late Fifties, and you see an example at the QET, opened in July 1959. The long beige building to the left of the theatre is the Main Post Office (1958). A kind of arts-and culture neighborhood is in genesis here: unseen just off to the left are the (now shuttered) Ford Theatre, the regional headquarters of the CBC, and the big main branch of the Vancouver Public Library.

The Old Sun Tower at Pender and Beatty, 2000.

The current owners have handsomely renovated this funky old favorite.

World Building (Old Sun Tower), 1920. Vancouver Public Library / 004309

What a life this famous building has had! We all call it the Old Sun Tower today, but it began life at Pender and Beatty Streets in 1912 as The World Building, named for the newspaper that L.D. Taylor had bought in 1905. Taylor did so well with the World (at one point it was running more display advertising than any other newspaper in North America) that he decided to put up a big building, with added office space, to house it. He made three fatal errors: he made it too big, he built it too far from the action, and it opened just as the local real estate market began a steep dive. Very few companies rented space in the building, and it eventually bankrupted Taylor.

Stand by this unique structure, and you'll see why it's one of the city's favorites: at 84 metres (276 feet) it was the tallest in the British Empire at the time, a title it held only briefly; its distinctive Beaux-Arts green copper dome (called "bombastic" by architectural historian Hal Kalman) can be seen from kilometres away; and there are nine lightly-clothed caryatids supporting the building. The "caryatids," concrete representations of beautiful women, are called the Nine Maidens.

The Sun bought the tower in 1937 (after it had had a short life as the Bekins Building), and published there until 1965. A young radio broadcaster named Jack Cullen remembers his first day on the job working for a station that rented space in the building: halfway through his show the building began to noticeably tremble. Jack bolted from his chair and made for the stairs. He was met by a startled custodian, who asked him why he was rushing downstairs so frantically. "There's an earthquake!" Cullen shouted, "It's shaking the whole building!" The custodian cocked an eyebrow at Jack. "Sonny," he said, "that's the presses rolling."

Aerial view over Yaletown's Roundhouse Mews to the south shore of False Creek, 2001. The red-roofed roundhouse is clearly visible at the corner of Davie and Pacific Boulevard.

Aerial view to the northeast over the rail yards and roundhouse on the north shore of False Creek, 1925. National Air Photo Library / BA12-12

YALETOWN

Aerial view to the north over False Creek to the downtown area, 1925
National Air Photo Library / BA10-25

Yaletown, the name given to the neighbourhood on the north shore of False Creek east of Granville Street, gets its name from the little CPR railway town of Yale. When the CPR extended its line from Port Moody to Vancouver in 1887, a lot of the railway's workers came from its operations in Yale. They congregated around the roundhouse, centre of the CPR's operations… and "Yaletown" was born. The warehouses that were built for their proximity to the railyards have today been converted into smart shops, intimate little restaurants, high-tech company headquarters, an extravagantly popular micro-brewery /restaurant and Urban Fare, a lavish and upscale "grocery" store. The combination of homely turn-of-the-century warehouses and other utilitarian buildings, the upscale businesses that now occupy them and the spanking new "smart" apartments and condos that abut them give Yaletown its unique flavour. The old roundhouse, once used for the repair and maintenance of CPR locomotives, has been transformed into a community centre and arts venue. On display here is Engine 374, which in May of 1887 brought the CPR's first passenger train into Vancouver.

FALSE CREEK

Panoramic view to the northwest over False Creek, Granville Island and the West End.

Old Hudson's Bay Company's Ft. Langley, C.1900. Vancouver Public Library / 013475

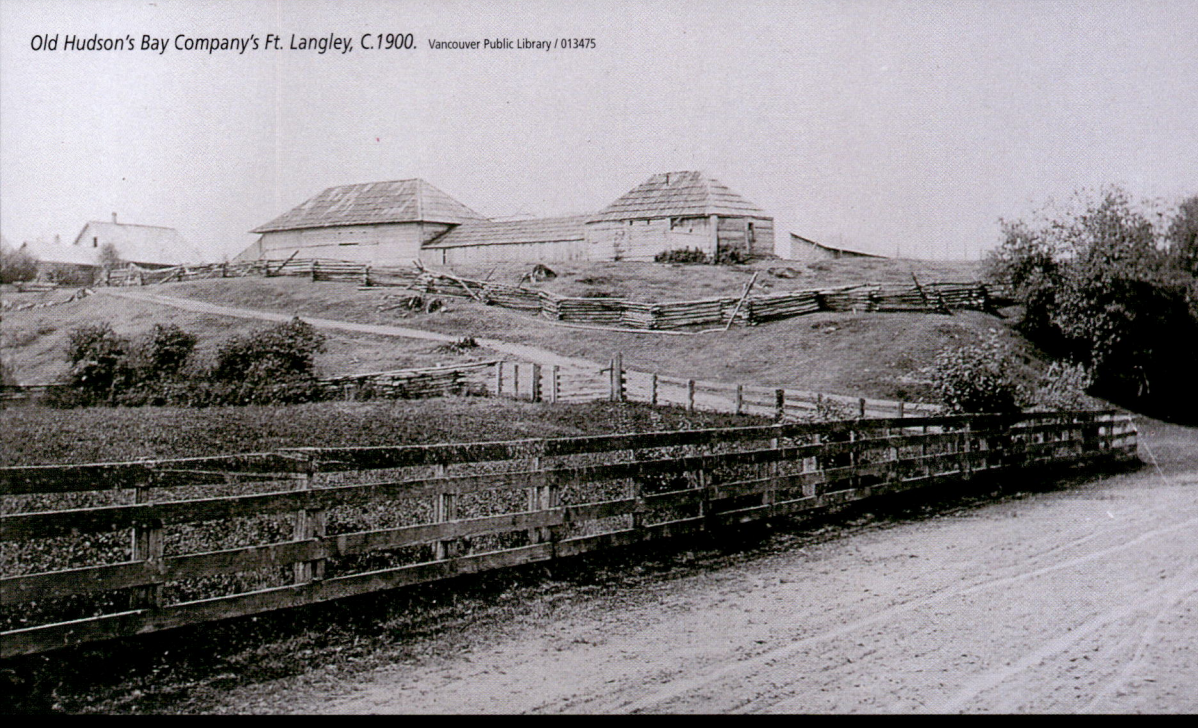

Ft. Langley

Here is where it all began. A modest start, it's true, but something remarkable would rise in its wake. This is Fort Langley in the 1870s, the second location for the Hudson's Bay Company's presence in the lower mainland of British Columbia. (The original fort, 35 kilometres downstream, had been abandoned in 1839 after 15 years.) Local native people, Kwantlen, Katzie, Kwikwitlem, brought furs to this fort and worked there, too, packing salted salmon. Many of the "Kanakas" (native Hawaiians) who worked here stayed on and married local native people. Their descendants remain among us today.

Fort Langley became the largest fish exporter on the Pacific coast of North America, with Hawaii a major market. Furs, fish and an agricultural industry capitalizing on the rich soil and abundant rainfall of the lower mainland were the economic catalysts that drove the pioneering economy of the region in these early days.

The fort, from which not a single shot was ever fired in anger, has been carefully restored and is now a major tourist attraction in the Fraser Valley. (It was in the "Big House" here that Governor James Douglas, on November 19, 1858 proclaimed the Crown Colony of British Columbia.) Fort Langley was established as a National Historic Park in May, 1955.

It was from this humble start that Greater Vancouver would emerge.

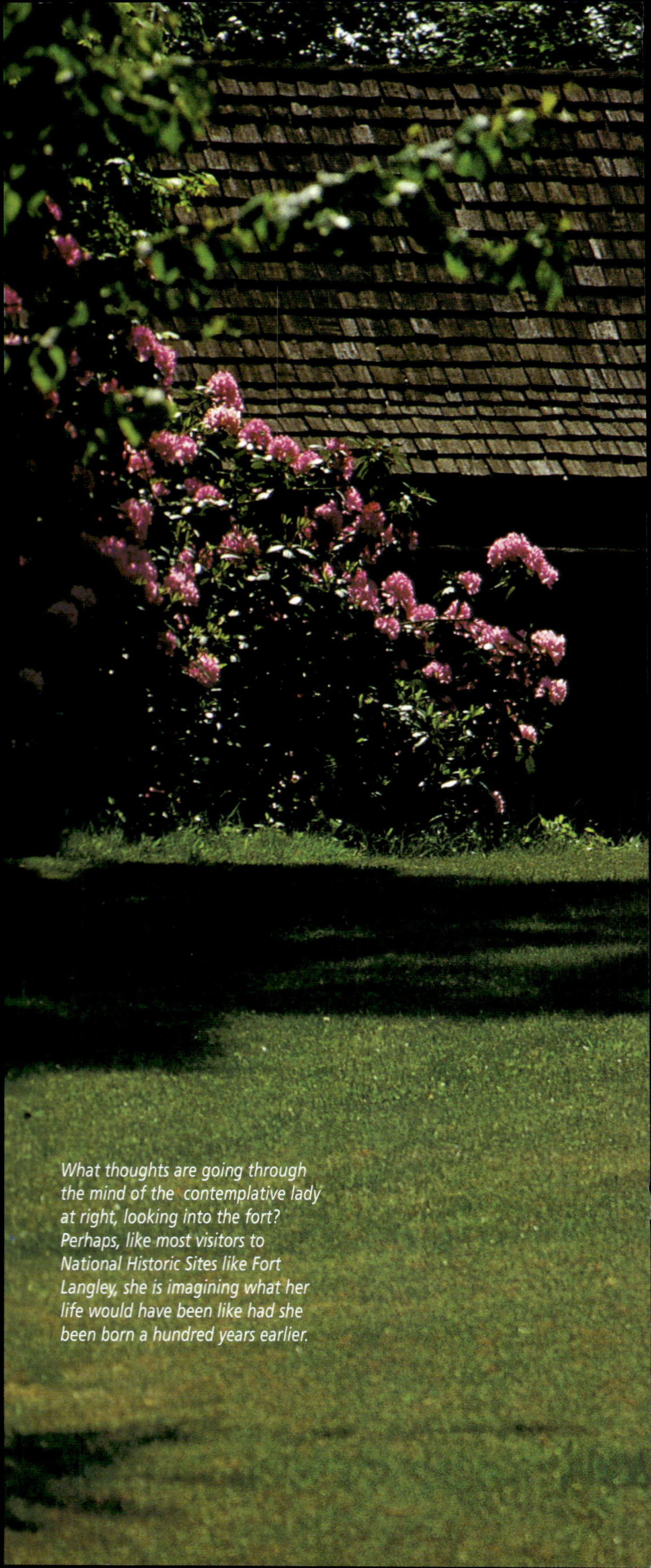

What thoughts are going through the mind of the contemplative lady at right, looking into the fort? Perhaps, like most visitors to National Historic Sites like Fort Langley, she is imagining what her life would have been like had she been born a hundred years earlier.

Servants' quarters believed to have been one of several used to house Hudson's Bay Company workers and their families.

The storehouse, built in the 1840s, is the only original building left on site. Used as a warehouse for most of the Hudson's Bay Company time period, it also saw service as a cooperage.

Boat and one of three bastions used as lookout stations and temporary housing.

When Colonel Richard Moody and his Royal Engineers examined the Fraser River in 1858, looking for high ground and good views of the river (in the event of an American invasion), they chose this spot. Moody named it Queensborough, in honor of Queen Victoria. The town was later renamed-- at the Queen's command--New Westminster.

View of New Westminster, 1860. Vancouver Public Library / 009940

View of New Westminster, 2001.

Beautiful photograph of a tranquil Fraser River and New Westminster the year before the fire of 1898. Vancouver Public Library / 008747

Aerial view of New Westminster on the north shore of the Fraser River. In the early days the center of town was at the foot of the hill, just : "west of the Pattullo Bridge, while today it is further west, at the foot of 8th Street. The blue roof of Westminster Quay and the riverboat casino are visible in this photograph and mark the spot where 8th Street ends at Columbia.

NEW WESTMINSTER

It was the river that created New Westminster, and that nourished her early life. When gold was discovered on the Fraser in 1858 it brought in battalions of prospectors, most American, who then worked the river farther and farther upstream. Rich strikes in the Cariboo in 1862 brought in more thousands. Steamships leaving New Westminster took supplies to the miners. But sailing ships worked here, too, and so did tugboats, paddle wheelers and freighters.

The inset photograph shows New Westminster in 1860, the year it was incorporated. It is the oldest incorporated municipality west of Ontario. (It began life as the capital city of the new colony of British Columbia, but lost that title to Victoria in 1868.)

The big photograph shows the busy port in 1897. The Westminster and Vancouver Tramway Company had established a line between Vancouver and "New West" some six years earlier in North America's first true "interurban" railway. The 45-minute trip took you through great stands of virgin timber that later became Burnaby. Fare was 75 cents return.

The Fraser was also home at this point to giant sturgeon. These behemoths are likely lurking beneath the placid waters of the Fraser in this very photograph. From the Columbian newspaper of August 14, 1897: "The largest of which any authenticated record has been kept was one weighing 1,387 lbs." Today the sturgeon have virtually vanished.

GREAT FIRE OF 1898

View west along Columbia Street the day after the great fire of 1898. Vancouver Public Library / 013260

It wasn't a carpet bombing, but the results were the same. A devastating fire struck New Westminster's downtown commercial core at 11 p.m. on Saturday, September 10, 1898. It had started in several tons of hay stored at the B&K wharf. The fire leaped from the warehouse there to the City Market next door. Just as it looked as if the city's fire department had the blaze under control, three sternwheelers moored at the wharf--the *Gladys,* the *Edgar* and the *Bon Accord*-- caught fire. The tide was running out strong, so the lashings of the vessels were cut to allow them to drift away. Tragically, a stiff wind pushed the boats against the wharves and they bumped crazily along, decks ablaze, setting fire to everything they touched. The CPR warehouse was engulfed, next came two large salmon canneries. "From the burning Columbian newspaper office," says a history of the New Westminster Fire Department, "the flames jumped to No. 1 Fire Hall opposite. The fire hall was a wood frame building situated between two brick buildings . . . it was consumed by the flames like a shingle in a stove." The YMCA was destroyed, then the library.

Just as people from New Westminster had helped Vancouver in the aftermath of its disastrous 1886 fire, so Vancouver came to the aid of the Royal City. Two hose reels and a crew under Vancouver fire chief John Carlisle arrived within 75 minutes to help fight the blaze.

When the last flames were extinguished it was realized the entire city from Royal Avenue to the waterfront had been ravaged. New Westminster's historic Chinatown was completely swept bare. This photo was taken the morning after the fire. No one was killed, but the property loss was estimated at $2.5 million. In 1898 dollars.

Warren "Whitey" Bernard standing on the same spot on 8th Street, 61 years after the famous photo was taken in 1940. He is holding a copy of Life Magazine open to the page carrying the timeless image.

WAIT FOR ME DADDY

Canada's most famous war photograph, a heart-stopping moment captured by the *Province's* chief photographer Claud Dettloff on October 10, 1940 as the British Columbia Regiment, Duke of Connaught's Own Rifles, are marching off to an uncertain future in the European theatre of the Second World War. Five-year-old Warren Bernard breaks away from his mother's hand and rushes to grasp the outstretched hand of his father, Pte. Jack Bernard.

The photograph, taken on 8th Street in New Westminster, was flashed all around the world within days. It appeared in Life Magazine, and has appeared in newspapers, magazines and books beyond counting.

It is a great photograph. And it has a happy ending: Jack Bernard returned from the war unscathed. He's gone now, but his son Warren--"Whitey" to his friends--lives and works today in Tofino.

"Wait for me Daddy". Soldiers of the B.C. Regiment, Duke of Connaught's Own Rifles parading down 8th Street to waiting trains and an uncertain future in the European theatre of the Second World War, 1940. Claud Detloff / Vancouver Public Library / 008516

BURNABY

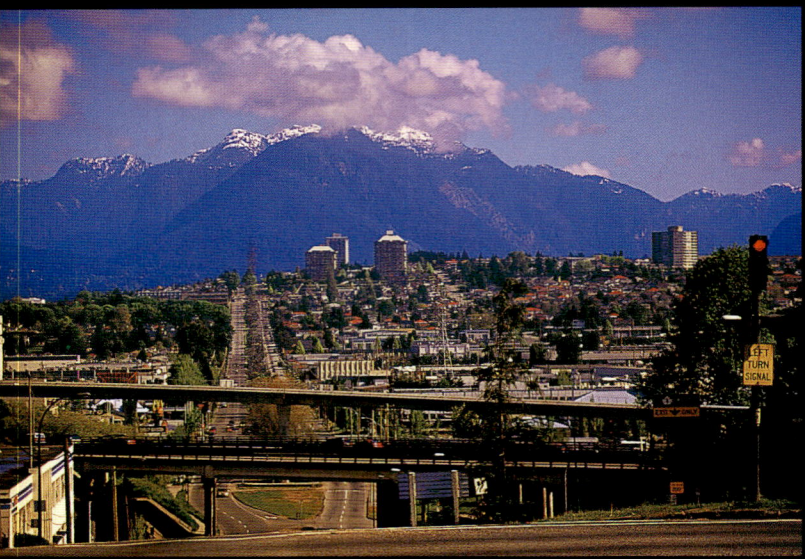

View looking north on Boundary Road from the Grandview Highway, 2001. The two overpasses carry the SkyTrain and Trans Canada Highway.

View north on Boundary Road in Burnaby on a slushy April morning in 1930. Burnaby is on the right and Vancouver begins to the left. Vancouver Public Library / 030640

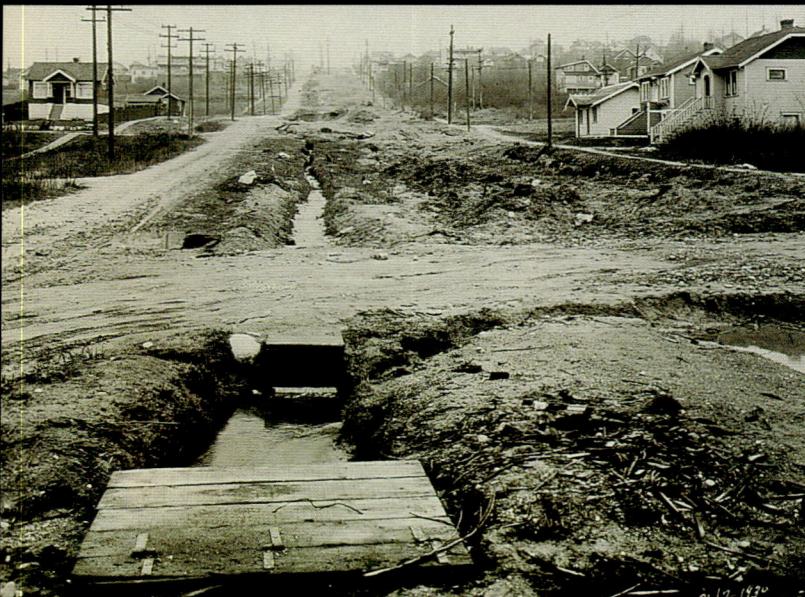

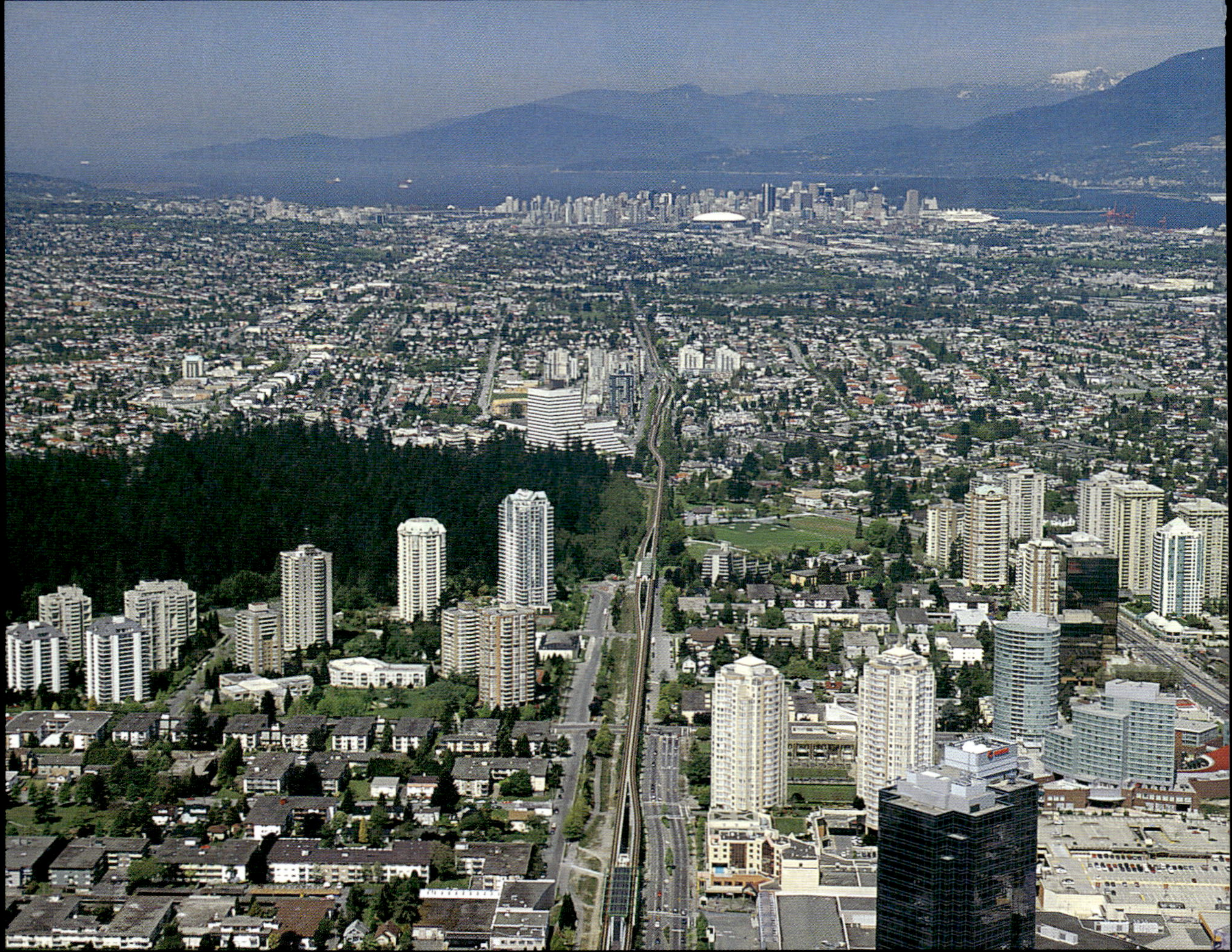

Aerial view looking west over Burnaby, along the SkyTrain right of way to downtown Vancouver, 2001.

Burnaby, the big city immediately east of Vancouver--the street that separates them, in fact, is called Boundary Road-is, at 107 square kilometres, almost as big as Vancouver (116 sq k) itself. It's mostly residential, but there are pockets of lively activity like the sprawling Kingsway shopping complex known as Metrotown. Burnaby was created in 1892 after traffic between Vancouver and New Westminster had sparked in 1891 the "Interurban," the rail transit system between the two bigger cities. (Today, Burnaby has more than three times the population of New West.) Today's SkyTrain follows the old Interurban route.

Another attraction here is Burnaby Village Museum, a turn-of-the-century replica of a small village. It's become a visitor attraction and a learning resource for school groups. It's also the home of a beautifully restored (and working) carousel.

Aerial view looking to the west along Kingsway from Royal Oak, 2001. That's Metrotown in the middle and the dark patch at the top is Central Park. On the right are two aerial views looking over Simon Fraser University atop its spectacular seeting on Burnaby Mountain. To the north is Indian Arm and the north shore mountains and to the west, Burrard Inlet and the city of Vancouver.

View to the north along Main Street from 7th Avenue to False Creek and the north shore mountains, 1889. Note how False Creek extends well to the east of Main Street. Vancouver Public Library / 000036

View to the north along Main Street from 7th Avenue to False Creek and the north shore mountains, 2001. The silver dome of Science World, visible just to the right of B.C. Place, marks the eastward extent of False Creek today.

The small 1889 photo at the top shows a long line of wooden planks leading down to False Creek. Today, that's Main Street. In the 1880s children in the Mount Pleasant neighborhood here were sometimes accompanied to school by their parents because of the bears, attracted to a local abundance of sweet blackberries. By 1905, when the larger picture was taken just two blocks farther south, at the corner of Westminster and 9th Avenues, the bears and the blackberries were gone.

Notice how, in the 1889 photograph, False Creek extends much farther inland? The eastern half of the Creek was filled in in 1921. Can you see the bridge, Vancouver's first, across the Creek?

MOUNT PLEASANT

Mount Pleasant has a lively historical society, and it was they who installed a plaque with that wonderful 1905 photograph at the same location—now known as Broadway and Main—at which it was taken almost a century earlier. (Imagine the wonder those 1905 folks would have felt at seeing a plaque with the 1889 shot. A mere 16 years separates the two pictures!)

View north across the busy intersection of Westminster (now Broadway) and Main, 1905. In 1912 the seven-storey Lee Building (visible in the contemporary photo) replaced the Methodist Church seen in the 1905 photograph. When completed it was the tallest building south of False Creek.

Philip Timms / Vancouver Public Library / 006718

CITY HALL

City Hall under construction, 1936. <small>Vancouver Public Library / 006718</small>

City Hall, 2001.

"It looks like a soap factory!" one unimpressed Vancouverite wrote to the newspaper in 1936 when Vancouver's brand-spanking-new City Hall was finished.

A lot of locals, most of them businessmen, protested the location of this new city hall in the former Strathcona Park in Mount Pleasant. It was a loooooong way from the downtown, and they didn't like the idea of having to travel all the way to Mount Pleasant. Why it's there: before 1929, if you had stood at Cambie and West 16th and faced south you would have had the City of Vancouver behind you. The Municipality of Point Grey (created in 1908) would be to your right, the Municipality of South Vancouver (1892) to your left. In 1929 both those places had amalgamated with Vancouver, and bumptious, aggressive Mayor Gerry McGeer wanted the symbolism of a city hall that was close to all three. Cynics said McGeer put it there because he was from Mount Pleasant.

Architectural historian Harold Kalman writes, "The hard-edged geometry of its dynamic cubic massing resembles the 'totalitarian classicism' seen in government buildings of the day from Munich to Moscow."

City Hall's famous clock can be seen from nearly all the city, and nearly all the city (right) can be seen from the roof of City Hall.

View of new City Hall from Yukon Street, 1937.
<small>Vancouver Public Library / 004693</small>

View north along Cambie to downtown Vancouver from the roof of City Hall, 1939.

View north along Cambie to downtown Vancouver from the roof of City Hall, 2001.

View over Fairview to False Creek and the downtown core of Vancouver, C.1911. Vancouver Public Library / 005207

Aerial view over Fairview to False Creek and the downtown core of Vancouver, C.1951. Vancouver Public Library

FAIRVIEW

The name of this neighborhood first appears on an 1890 map of Vancouver, and we can thank CPR surveyor and land commissioner Lauchlan Hamilton for that. In the summer of 1887 Hamilton stepped out of his canoe into the forest on the southern slope and looked back. The little hamlet across False Creek basked in the sun, and in the distance the imposing mountains of the Coast Range loomed. "I'll call this place Fairview," Hamilton said.

Twenty or so years later (c. 1911), in a photograph taken around Oak Street and West 12th Avenue, Fairview was, as you see to the left, nicely settled. The CPR owned a lot of property in the area, and they wanted people to settle here, so they offered the New Westminster and Vancouver Tramway Co. a number of free lots along 9th Avenue (now Broadway) to induce the company to put in a tram line. Done! By the end of 1891 the Fairview Beltline was in, and people began moving into the neighborhood. They could get to the downtown core via the first Granville Street Bridge (1889) or the brand-new (1891) Cambie Street Bridge. That 1889 bridge crossed a couple of sandbars in False Creek, sandbars that by 1916 had been filled in and built upon to create Granville Island.

Sixty years after Hamilton's canoe trip (1952, lower left) Fairview's view wasn't quite so fair. The Coast Mountains still loomed impressively, but were now usually viewed through a plume of industrial smoke. There were factories along the southern bank of False Creek, and Granville Island was one big industrial complex. (By 1930, says writer Catherine Gourley, there were 1,200 people working in the island's factories, "churning out steel rivets, band saws, anvils, bolts, cement, paint, barrels, rope, boilers and chains.")

1952 was the year the last of the "Fairview Shacks" was torn down. These dank, somber buildings--formerly used by Vancouver General Hospital--were once the home of the University of British Columbia! For 13 years, from 1912 to 1925, students justifiably grumbled and carped about having to study in the shacks, until a famous student protest called "The Great Trek." On October 28, 1922 more than 1,200 fed-up students marched from Fairview to the undeveloped UBC land at Point Grey. The provincial government finally got off its duff and began to build a proper campus. It opened in 1925.

View north over Fairview from the Vancouver General Hospital's Jim Pattison Pavilion, 2001.

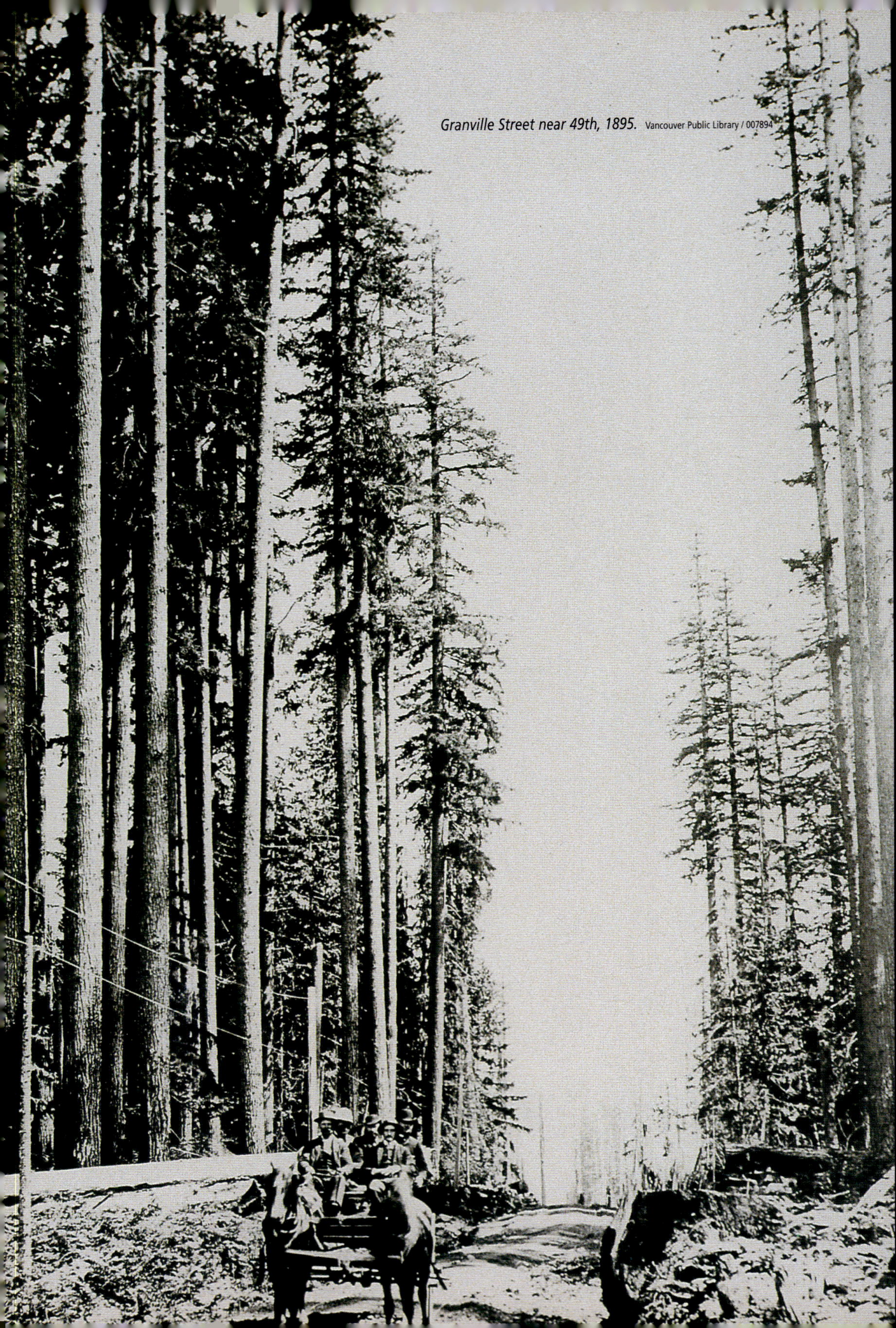

Granville Street near 49th, 1895. Vancouver Public Library / 007894

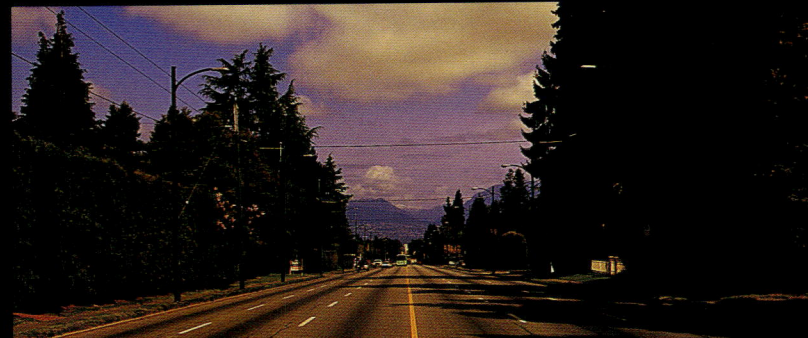

It's one hundred years later and Granville Street is a little wider, the trees are a little shorter and it is traffic–rather than mud up to your axle–that will delay your drive into Vancouver in the 21st century.

We went over to Vancouver once in a while, driving up Granville Street, as it is now called, but then it was just a slit in the forest; a solid wall of trees on both sides from Eburne to False Creek with timber so tall you had to look straight up to see the sky. We went over to Vancouver on the first day of July, 1890, and the mud on Granville Street was up to the hubs. The sun could not get in to dry the road - the trees were so tall. The road was no wider than a wagon, and, every half mile or so there was a little space, somewhat wider, where wagons could pass.

Mrs. H.E. Campbell, quoted in J.S. Matthews,
Early Vancouver, volume 1, number 152.

Fifteen years have passed since the picture at left was taken and the motor car is about to displace the horse–but not right away. It looks like the horse on the right is being prepared to pull this realtor's car out of the muddy ditch in which it is stuck. The year is aabout 1910 and the location is near 4th and Waterloo in Kitsilano. Vancouver Public Library / 013170

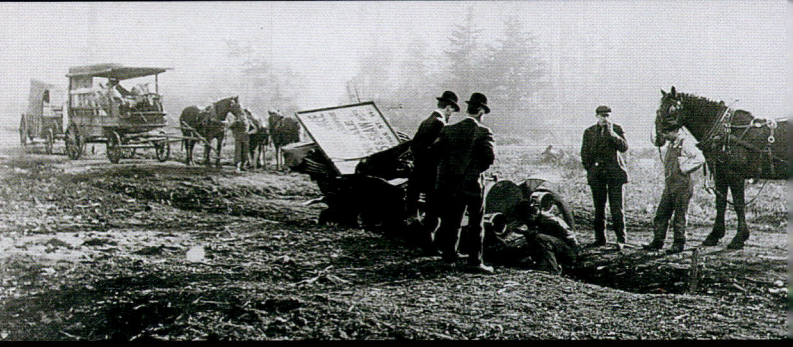

Manicured gardens near the Bloedel Conservatory in beautiful Queen Elizabeth Park. This is one of Vancouver's most popular parks for wedding pictures and is so large that it features a pitch and putt golf course.

Aerial view of University of British Columbia campus on Point Grey, 1925. Point Atkinson and Howe Sound can be seen in the background of this wonderful photo.
ational Air Photo Library / BA12-2

UNIVERSITY OF
BRITISH COLUMBIA

he sprawling University of British Columbia campus, at the tip of Point Grey (right), is a very, very busy place. More than 29,000 undergraduates are down there, more than 6,000 graduate students, over 2,000 international students from more than 100 countries… and they're learning from nearly 2,000 faculty, supported by more than 12,000 non-faculty staff.

When UBC began in 1915 it had 379 students, toiling at their studies in gloomy quarters called the "Fairview Shacks." It took a famous student protest march (1922's 'Great Trek') to spur the provincial government to build the promised Point Grey campus. That opened in 1925 (above), ten years after the university started.

here are lots of attractions here: the Nitobe Gardens, the world-famed Museum of Anthropology, the Chan Centre for the Performing Arts … and acting as a "green belt" between Vancouver and the campus, the spectacular Pacific Spirit Regional Park

Aerial view of University of British Columbia campus on Point Grey, 2001. This is a southeasterly perspective, exactly the opposite to the 1925 image at left, and provides a look at (left to right) Spanish Banks, most of Kitsilano and the airport.

Downtown

Let's take an imaginative leap here. We've reserved that small log on the left for you to sit on, and we're taking you back in time to 1886, more than a century ago—with this book on your lap. You call to the gentlemen in the background to lay down their tools for a moment, and ask them and the children to gather round. It takes a few moments for that fellow standing on the giant log to get down and join the group. You open your book to this page and point to the picture on the right. "That," you tell them, "is what a birds eye view of this spot will look like 115 years from now. It is May 15, 2001 and you're looking west along Georgia Street and Downtown Vancouver"

They would likely find you hard to believe.

Who could blame them? We'd doubt our eyes at being shown this corner in 2115 AD on a holograph or whatever medium will exist then.

Georgia and Granville, 1886, future site of The Bay.
The tree-line in the background is the future Burrard Street
to the northwest J.A. Brock / Vanvouver Public Library / 013185

The tree-line in the background of the old photo has been transformed into gleaming office towers by 2001. Georgia Street can be seen slicing straight up the photo on its left side, just to the right of the Colosseum-like building (bottom left) that is home to the new Vancouver Public Library, source of many of the archival images in this book including the one at left. Directly across from the tall building with the Scotia Bank logo stands The Bay. This is the corner of Georgia and Granville, the location where the beautiful photograph at left was taken.

We'd have questions to ask of these folk: do you happen to have a copy of the *Vancouver Weekly Herald* and *North Pacific News,* Vancouver's first newspaper? (Issue #1: January 15, 1886.) Were you at the dock when the first inward cargo to the port, tea from China, arrived July 26? Can you explain why British Columbia is now charging Chinese men a $50 head tax (that can be four months' pay)? And to the kids, How come your Daddy lets you play around these big, dangerous logs?

And they'd have questions for us: how many horses are there in Vancouver in the 21st century? Is the city a lot noisier? Have you heard about that brand-new drink, Coca-Cola? (They started selling it May 8th!) How many women have been mayor of Vancouver? The kids might ask, Do children still have to go to school?

It's time to go. "But just before I leave, little lady, I want to tell you one more thing. On the very spot where you are standing, the Hudson's Bay Company will have a big, big store where you can buy clothes, and perfume, and tools, and watches, and furniture, and stoves and refrigerators, and have your photograph taken, and your hair done, and eyeglasses fitted, and eat in a big restaurant and buy a television set and… What's that? What's 'television'? Well… it's sort of like radio with pictures. Radio? Well…"

1909 was a banner year for these five blocks of West Hastings. Here we see the Winch Building, Post Office and the Dominion Trust buildings in various stages of construction. Vancouver Public Library / 005254

Similar view east along Hastings, 2001.

Two buildings that needed saving, and got it. Closest to us, in this photograph taken about 1910, is the Winch Building. Architect Thomas Hooper designed this building for R.V. Winch, who had made his fortune in the fishing business. (Winch, who had run away from home in Cobourg, Ontario when he was 16, was 31 when he got here. He was able to enjoy looking at his building for more than 40 years, dying in 1952 at 90.) Local architects esteem this handsome structure.

Just beyond it, and still waiting for its famous clock to be installed, is the new post office, on the northwest corner of Hastings and Granville, replacing a smaller one a block away at Pender and Granville. On February 28, 1910 the World bid a fond farewell to the latter. "The

old building," the paper said, "has ceased to be the sorting house for tidings of good and ill, and soon its associations with the curt business letter and the scented billet doux will be forgotten…" And the paper welcomes the new, "the palatial building… a landmark, a monument of chiselled stone and massive rounded pillars, that caused the visitor to be impressed with Vancouver's power and prosperity." Today both buildings are part of Sinclair Centre, the glossy office and retail complex.

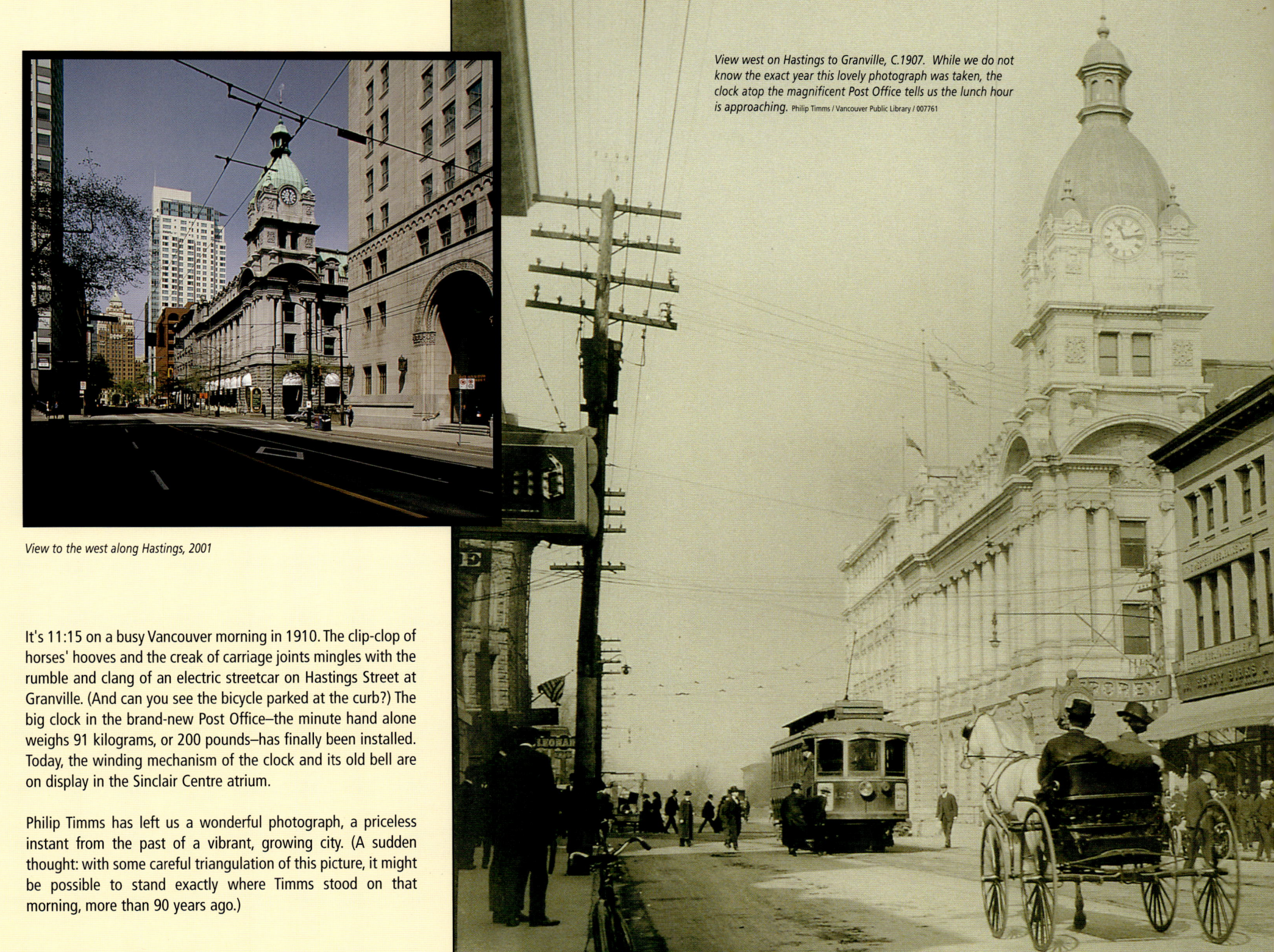

View west on Hastings to Granville, C.1907. While we do not know the exact year this lovely photograph was taken, the clock atop the magnificent Post Office tells us the lunch hour is approaching. Philip Timms / Vancouver Public Library / 007761

View to the west along Hastings, 2001

It's 11:15 on a busy Vancouver morning in 1910. The clip-clop of horses' hooves and the creak of carriage joints mingles with the rumble and clang of an electric streetcar on Hastings Street at Granville. (And can you see the bicycle parked at the curb?) The big clock in the brand-new Post Office—the minute hand alone weighs 91 kilograms, or 200 pounds—has finally been installed. Today, the winding mechanism of the clock and its old bell are on display in the Sinclair Centre atrium.

Philip Timms has left us a wonderful photograph, a priceless instant from the past of a vibrant, growing city. (A sudden thought: with some careful triangulation of this picture, it might be possible to stand exactly where Timms stood on that morning, more than 90 years ago.)

View to the southeast across the intersection of Granville and Hastings, 1926. In the contemporary photo below our photographer took his cue from the shooter of the old photo above, placing himself in a slightly different vantage point on the very same Post Office.

The bank as temple. This is one of the handsomest buildings in the city, originally known as the Bank of Commerce, at the southeast corner of Hastings and Granville. The picture dates from 1926. It happens that when this bank opened in 1908 it was directly across Hastings Street from the elegant Birks jewelry store. (Birks, established in Montreal in 1879, had come to Vancouver in 1907 and purchased George Trorey's jewelry store at the northeast corner of Hastings and Granville. Trorey stayed on as manager.)

The purchase included a tall, handsome sidewalk clock (built in England in 1905, with a wooden movement that works to this day). You can see it in the picture above, when it was still Trorey's Clock. After 1907, it became known as the Birks Clock, and became a Vancouver icon. So, when Birks moved November 8th, 1913 into its own (now vanished) building at Georgia and Granville, it brought the clock along and installed it at that corner. "Meet you at the Birks Clock" must have been said a half-million times over the next eight decades.

On October 23, 1994 Birks moved again—this time into that handsome Bank of Commerce Building, right across the street from their original store. And of course the famous clock moved, too. They wind it every Tuesday morning, just like Big Ben.

Vancouverites employing their best defensive weapon against their traditional foe at the corner of Granville and Hastings, 2001.

We can now confirm the rumors: it rains in Vancouver. We submit as proof this photograph taken at Hastings and Granville in 1905. Actually, there are more umbrellas down than up, so a shower has likely just ended.

This photograph, damp as it is, shows Vancouver at a time when it was booming: as mentioned elsewhere in this book the population jumped from 27,000 in 1901 to 100,000 in 1911, so in this picture we're right in the middle of that climb. Bank clearings were way up, customs receipts were up, building permits jumped in value by a third in one year and civic election candidates were calling for the city's streets to be extended right out to all the city's boundaries. There were 50 realtors in the city in 1900, some 650 by 1910!

A fellow named Campbell who had won a city lot at the northwest corner of Pender and Abbott with a $1 raffle ticket just before the 1886 fire held on to it until 1908 when he sold it for $50,000. To put that into perspective, a laborer at the time made 31.25 cents an hour for a 48-hour week, so that $50,000 was equivalent to 64 years of work. Not a bad return. Bring on the rain! Who cares?!

Pedestrians on Hastings reflected in the rainy sidewalk on Hastings, 1905.
Vancouver Public Library / 005222

View east along Hastings from atop the Guinness Tower, 2001.

121

A view south along Granville at Pender, 1906. Vancouver Public Library / 005226

Almost seventy-five years have passed and while fashions have changed, the sunshine and many of the fine old buildings on this stretch of Granville survive.

There's a vaguely European flavor to the 1906 urban landscape on the left. Unless you knew better, you could be persuaded that this was a city in France or the U.K. A distinctive West Coast style for our buildings is still some years away. Still, there's a solidity to the city's architectural infrastructure that speaks of confidence, maybe even a little arrogance. Remember the World's reference to "Vancouver's power and prosperity."

Meantime, over there on the right, striding confidently along Granville Street on a sunny day in 1928, these two ladies in their stylish cloche hats look breezy and liberated. Not quite. In April of this very year the Supreme Court of Canada ruled that women were not "persons." The judges expanded on the judgement, ruling that "by the common law of England, women were under a legal incapacity to hold public office."

So it isn't just our streets and buildings that have undergone dramatic change. That paternalistic ruling was overturned the following year, and so these two women would become eligible, if they cared to, to sit in the Senate.

The car was becoming more common on Vancouver streets. This is the year the city's first automatic traffic light signals went in (at the corner of Main and Hastings). People drove downtown to see them! There is ample photographic proof that uniformed policemen performed this important function at major intersections… which they do these days if the power goes out.

There's a buzz to daily life here in 1928, an effervescence, helped by the knowledge that in a short while Vancouver, by amalgamating with Point Grey and South Vancouver, will soon become the third largest city in Canada.

But ominous clouds are gathering. Next year will be 1929 and on faraway Wall Street in New York City the stock market is in for a very big, and very nasty, surprise.

A view to the north along Granville Street from the roof of the Scotia Tower on Georgia, 2001.

Vancouver women had at last succumbed to the craze for bobbed hair. Men commented that it was the first time they had ever seen women's ears on the street.

From "Twenty Years Ago",
The Vancouver Sun,
5 September 1946.

View north on Granville from Pender, 1928. Leonard Frank / Vancouver Public Library / 005254

Did those three schoolgirls just get off that streetcar now heading north on Granville from Robson Street? And if so, where are they going? Alas, it's more than 95 years ago and we can only speculate. Just as we can only guess at whatever 1906 headlines are on that newspaper the boy's carrying. Could they be reporting train robber Bill Miner's capture up in Quilchena? (The "Grey Fox" was nabbed by the RCMP on May 14.) Maybe the April 18 San Francisco earthquake is the big story. Vancouver Public Library / 005227

Tourism is a major factor–perhaps the biggest of them all–in the Vancouver economy today, but even in 1905 it was making its contribution. Here we are outside the offices of the Vancouver Tourist Association on Granville Street as a Tally Ho wagon drawn by four horses prepares to depart with a group of tourists. The building behind the woman and child is the Hudson's Bay store, there since 1893. Philip Timms / Vancouver Public Library / 005235

View north on Granville from Georgia, 2001

View north on Granville from Georgia, C.1905. Vancouver Public Library / 005205

"Hang on to Mommy, dear, the streetcar's coming!"

The streetcar shaped Vancouver, just as it shaped other young cities of the time. It allowed a lot of people who worked downtown or in industrial areas to afford their own homes in distant, less expensive places. In many older cities workers lived in central-core tenements or over shops. The railway (you can see the CPR station at the north end of Granville in this scene, about 1905) made the city, but the streetcar played a big part in its development.

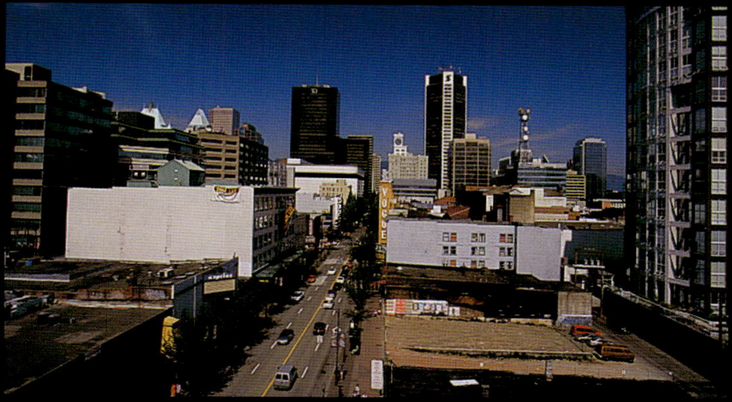

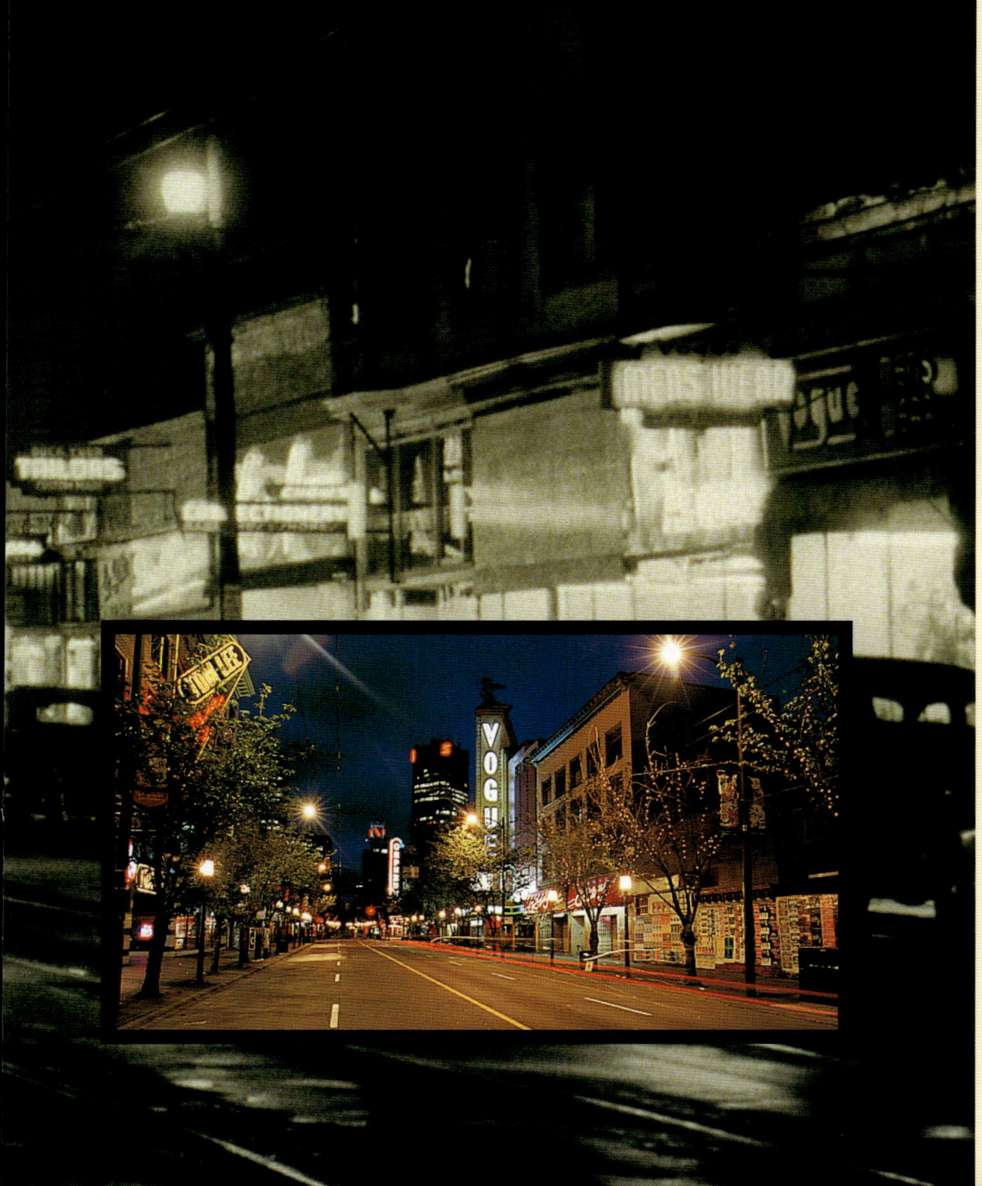

Vancouver Public Library / 006437

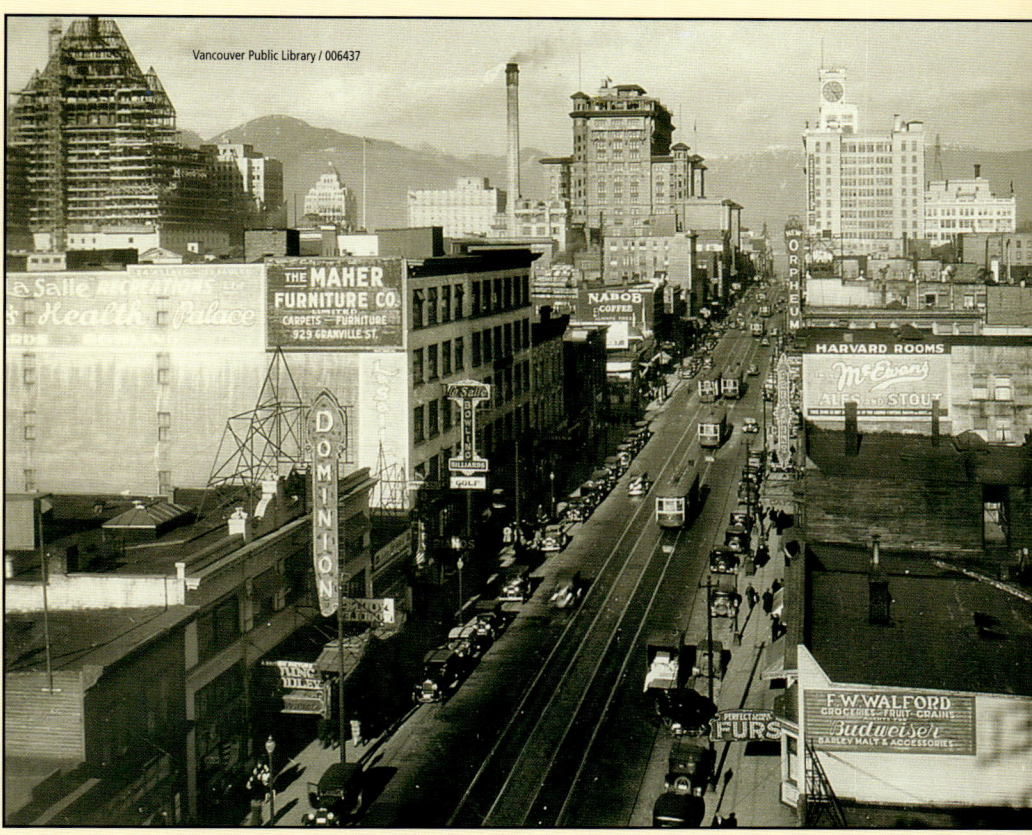

The first neon sign on Granville Street flickered on in 1925. The street was ablaze by the 1950s, when Vancouver had more neon footage than any city in the world outside of Shanghai– more than 18,000 signs! Can you spot the big Shell sign atop the Vancouver Block in this 1950s shot? The best sign was the Orpheum Theatre's, "combining ruby red, white and blue neon inside a gracefully curved frame of moving incandescemt bulbs". Less than 20 years later most of Granville's blazing neon was gone, and only recently has it started making a modest return.

The picture above shows Granville about 1932. The Great Depression had settled like a sodden shroud on the city. Thousands of us were on relief (34,000 at the peak), and hundreds more were riding the rods into town on every freight train. (The author's father was one of them.) Historian Alan Morley counted 1,250 men in the breadline at First United Church. A symbol of the economic downturn: the unfinished form of the Hotel Vancouver.

Spencer's Department Store (bottom left) on Hastings Street is festooned with flags to honor the visit May 25, 1939 to Vancouver of King George VI and Queen Elizabeth (now the Queen Mother). This tour provided Canada with one of the greatest demonstrations of national unity in her history. Four days earlier in Ottawa, the King had dedicated the capital's new War Memorial in honor of the 60,000 Canadians lost in the Great War. On September 1st, 1939, or 99 days after this photograph was taken, Hitler's troops invaded Poland and the Second World War began.

The Second World War ended August 14, 1945 and Vancouver—along with the rest of the Allied nations—erupted in jubilation. There were a few Stars and Stripes being waved along with Union Jacks by those kids on Granville Street. The B.C. Electric's sleek new trolleys, sharing the tracks with older models, crept carefully through boisterous crowds lining every downtown street. Horns blew, factory whistles shrilled, kids cheered, people sang . . . and vast waves of relief and exhilaration swept the city. Now we would wait for our veterans to return, and begin to plan postwar readjustment. One example: at the University of British Columbia enrolment jumped from 2,900 in 1944 to 7,300 in 1946.

Veterans parading along Granville on Armistice Day, November 11th, 1918. Vancouver Public Library / 006647

View west along Hastings from Richards, 1939. Vancouver Public Library / 007883

Inside Spencer's store in 1944, with the war five years old. Vancouver's citizens are urged to send parcels to the men and women overseas. W.J. Moore / Vancouver Public Library / 071014

They are too near
To be great
But our children
Shall understand
When and how our
Fate was changed
And by whose hand.

Rudyard Kipling   1917

Kiplings' words appear on the wall of the Memorial Chamber in the Peace Tower of the Parliament buildings. They might have been written—in fact, were written—about the veterans in the photograph at top left, opposite, celebrating the end of the war. It's November 11, 1918 on Granville Street at Georgia, and British Columbia and Canada and the world have finally emerged from four years of the hell of the First World War.

VJ celebrations sweep Vancouver, 1945

Vancouver Public Library / 068701E

Jack Lindsay / Vancouver Public Library / 039005

Vancouver Public Library / 044918

VJ celebrations sweep Vancouver, 1945

129

At sea level from the north, at 2,000 feet from the south, morning, afternoon or night, the city of Vancouver loves the camera.

Vancouver is an island completely surrounded by envy.

Unknown

BURRARD STREET
AND BRIDGE.
LEONARD FRANK

Early on in the process of capturing the contemporary versions of many of the archival images I ran into problems. The splendid Leonard Frank photograph above, taken in 1932 from the still unfinished Hotel Vancouver, is a case in point. Arriving at the spot on the roof of the hotel I thought Frank would have utilized, it was no surprise to discover that his old view southward to the Burrard Bridge was now completely obscured by the proliferation of new buildings the intervening 70-odd years had generated. Next stop was the roof of the Park Plaza at Burrard and Dunsmuir. This spot offered up some splendid views, like the one below which includes the Hotel Vancouver, but still no bridge. A quick trip down to the bridge itself and, standing in the middle, the only building I could see from my target area was the top of the Scotia Tower on Georgia Street. Once again, some beautiful vistas and, if you look closely just to the right of the page break on the large image, you have a view straight down the centreline of the bridge. *John McQuarrie, Photographer*

Another interesting aspect of the city that becomes evident in the large view is the shortage of green space in the downtown core. Perhaps early city planners thought that with Stanley Park, and the vast green spaces surrounding English Bay, Vancouverites could do without when it came to their business district. But a valiant and successful resolve to reverse this trend can be seen in the park-like setting of Robson Square between the old and new courthouses. The three small inset photos reflect the park-like setting to be found there.

Kitsilano Beach, formerly Greers Beach,, July 1st, 1905. City of Vancouver Archives / BE P50 N23

Kitsilano beach, formerly Greer's Beach, 1909. City of Vancouver Archives / BE P122 N73

THE BAY KITSILANO. B.C.

KITSILANO BEACH

The 1905 photograph of Kits Beach above almost looks like a Winslow Homer painting. To the left, Kits Beach, four years later, a photo taken from west of the foot of Yew Street. Now the style, at least where the people in the latter picture appear, approaches French impressionism!

This is the area once known as Greer's Beach, for Sam Greer, the squatter who lived here with his family until evicted by the CPR in 1887. He didn't go without a fight: in one of the more celebrated of Vancouver's dramatic incidents, Sam shot the sheriff sent to evict him. Sam spent some time in jail, and the sheriff survived.

"The proof," comments the late city archivist Major Matthews regarding the photo to the left, "that this is the summer of 1909 is that all the campers' tents have gone, not allowed for sanitary reasons after 1908 …

It's 1928 at Kits Beach and local citizens are taking the sun... very cautiously. The ladies are thoroughly covered in this Leonard Frank photograph, the men's fedoras tightly clamped onto their heads. Can you imagine what these upright folk of 75 years ago would make of our bikini-clad and Speedo-sporting sun seekers today?
City of Vancouver Archives / BE 15 N99

This gentleman has discovered one of the perfect benches to watch the people going by, the tide coming in and the sun dropping into Howe Sound.

Kitsilano Beach and street car loop, 1931 Leonard Frank / Vancouver Public Library / 006116

There was an earlier building on the site of this first Park Board Bathhouse, a large rambling structure, privately owned, used as a primitive dance hall." There were boats for hire then, and a log float, later demolished. Just beyond the line of trees in the background was property subdivided into residential lots by the CPR and opened for settlement the year this later photo was taken. "Behind the bathhouse," Matthews continues, "was, until 1913, a swamp with muskrats in the sloughs. It was filled in to the depth of 13 feet at Maple Street, three feet at Arbutus." The fill, incidentally, was sand dredged up from False Creek. (Note to readers who live on Maple or Arbutus Streets today: does your house seem just a trifle shaky?)

Matthews comments that in the half-century preceding the 1909 photo, the shoreline has moved westward "at least 250 feet" because of sand washed in from Spanish Banks.

All the more room in 1931 for that little streetcar (upper right) to come clanging into the loop.

Indulge in fantasy. See that motorcycle and sidecar parked across the street from Kits Pool? Imagine yourself astride that machine with your Significant Other seated next to you . . . and off you go, gliding down these quiet 1931 streets on a wide-eyed journey of exploration. (Your motorcycle's quiet, too. This is a fantasy, after all.) The Burrard Bridge is visible in the blue distance, but you can't cross her yet. The bridge doesn't open until Dominion Day, 1932.

Wonder what those folks on the sidewalk are talking about? (Look closer at this photograph and you'll see a little drama unfolding. Standing between the cars just to the left of the couple on the sidewalk are two police officers, one with his horse. Now look at the intersection at lower left: there's a speeding car heading in the officers' direction, and coming dangerously close to the vehicle making the right-hand turn onto Cornwall. Wonder what happened next? On second thought, maybe your fantasy shouldn't include a trip on that motorcycle. It probably belongs to the second cop!)

Kitsilano pool and beach, 1931. Trials for the Los Angeles Olympic Games were held in the Kits pool and the Burrard Street Bridge can be seen in the background, ready for its official opening July 1st, 1932 W.J. Moore / City of Vancouver Archives / BE P22 N5

The appearance of the park and pool area, shown here in 2001, remains largely unchanged from 1931. But the view of Vancouver's West End, visible across English Bay, shows considerable change.

Early morning tranquility of pool in Kitsilano Beach Park.

Broad sandy beach in Kitsilano Park could pass for a Caribbean tropical setting on this beautiful sunny afternoon.

Lifeguard using binoculars to keep track of kayakers and wind surfers enjoying the sparkling waters of English Bay.

Beach volleyball is very popular across Canada and few settings can match Kitsilano Beach for this thriving sport.

139

Aerial view to the northwest over present day Hadden Park to the West End and downtown Vancouver, 1925. Vancouver Public Library / 013171

Kitsilano is still raw by 1925, but developing rapidly. The combination of scenic English Bay to the west and industry-rich False Creek to the right brought an astonishing mix of people to the area, some well-to-do, some gritty laborers, giving it a vitality and character all its own. There are many who, to this day, say Kits is the best of all Vancouver neighborhoods. That broad stretch of land in mid-photo is Hadden Park today, home of the Maritime Museum. In the distance, across the entrance to False Creek, the West End and Downtown.

It was the streetcar that made Kits work. Residences popped up all along the new lines, and shops popped up next to them. In the two photos at right we see workers preparing the new 4th Street line and then, the inaugural run in October of 1909. For those Kits residents who don't recognize the location, it's 4th Street near Waterloo

In the 1960s, Kitsilano will become Vancouver's hippie haven. Some of the flavor of those turbulent times lingers on to this day.

The photo at right shows Hadden Park, home to the Vancouver Museum, Pacific Space Centre and the Vancouver Maritime Museum. It is here that the famous RCMP vessel, *St Roch*–first ship to navigate the Northwest Passage in both directions–is on permanent display.

Vancouver Public Library / 013176

Aerial view to the north west over present day Hadden Park to the West End and downtown, Vancouver, 2001.

Prior Street streetcar barn of the Vancouver Electric Railway and Light Company, 1894. Vancouver Public Library / 019783A

TRANSIT

In 1889 Vancouver's earliest transit entrepreneurs were planning a system of horse-drawn streetcars. A latecomer to the group, a gentleman named Henry McKee, informed them that Victoria was planning an electrical system. Was Vancouver, which had pretensions of being the province's major city, going to let Victoria lead the way? Of course not! So the Vancouver Street Railway Co. quickly arranged a merger with the Vancouver Electric Illuminating Co., and the Vancouver Electric Railway and Light Co. was born. Six electric cars were ordered. Fifteen years later, as you see in this terrific 1904 photo taken at Hastings and Homer, the system (now the B.C. Electric Railway Co.) was in full swing.

Streetcars passing street sweeper on Hastings and Homer, 1904. Philip Timms / Vancouver Public Library / 005211

SkyTrain crossing Fraser River at New Westminster enroute to Vancouver, 2001.

Interurban Car 1231 of The Downtown Historic Railway on one of its regular runs between Science World and Granville Island. Operating summer weekends and holidays, the Transit Museum Society provides a rare opportunity to step back in time aboard a real working interurban car.

SkyTrain arriving at Main Street Station, 2001.

The streetcar snaked out into undeveloped regions of the lower mainland and brought new homes and businesses in its wake. The growth of Vancouver would not have been possible without it. The 1891 creation of the "Interurban," the first truly interurban transit system in North America, linked Vancouver with New Westminster. By 1905 BCER tracks had been extended to Stanley Park, Davie, Robson, Main, Fraser, Commercial Drive and Kitsilano. By 1914 there were 232 cars.

Rails were laid through neighboring cities and the system thrived. By the end of World War II, a gradual shift to electric trolleys began, and motorized buses began to replace the railed systems. On April 24, 1955 the last streetcar ran. By the 1960s--as more and more people moved to the suburbs--the family car began to supplant the transit system.

The 1986 creation of SkyTrain--the light-rapid transportation system that runs without on-board personnel--made travel from Vancouver through Burnaby and New Westminster faster and more convenient, with a new line to Coquitlam in the offing, but in terms of the number of users public transit today is a pale shadow of the day when virtually everyone took the streetcar.

Bird's eye view of Burrard Station from atop the Park Plaza, 2001.

ENGLISH BAY

On the sunny slope which dips with gentle undulations into the golden west, and commands an exquisite panoramic eyeshot of the Gulf of Georgia, the mountains of Vancouver Island and Howe Sound, softly blue in the enchanted distance, the well-to-do of Vancouver have pitched their tents and settled down amid surroundings the most salubrious and beautiful. Here they have transformed what was, ten years ago, a virgin forest, where the salmon berry, the salal, the huckleberry and succulent skunk cabbage flourished in prodigal luxuriance in the fat and sappy soil, into a West End of which any city in all America might be proud

The Vancouver Daily Province, 10 November 1900.

Panoramic view of English Bay, the Strait of Georgia and the distant mountains of Vancouver Island from the appropriately named Sunset Beach, 2000.

Despite Vancouver's temperate climate, the waters of English Bay have always been a touch too cool for most. Back in 1907, the locals were quite content to sit on the beach, decently clad from neck to knees, or stroll along the 300 feet of the magnificent English Bay Pier. There was a very popular roller skating rink on the shore at the entrance to the pier. And we can be sure lifeguard Joe Fortes is among that sprinkling of people splashing around: Joe went down to his beloved English Bay every day without fail. He drank, for his health, a cup of its salt water daily. Sadly, the old pier was demolished in 1938. Not a few people have suggested it would be a wonderful idea to rebuild it!

View east over the famous English Bay Pier to Sunset Beach and the West End, 1907.
That's Davie Street disappearing over the hill on the left.

'Our Bathing Beach', English Bay, 2001. A comparison of these two photos shows that a fairly broad stretch of land has been reclaimed from the Bay since 1906.

Vancouver Police Constable keeping a sharp lookout for City Bylaw #135 violators.
Photo courtesy of Vancouver Police Museum

My, how times have changed! Back around the time (1906) Philip Timms was taking this photograph, a letter appeared in the Vancouver Daily Province from a young lady who wrote: "My country visit has left me badly tanned. I would like to have it taken off before school commences. Can you give me any assistance?" This picture of English Bay visitors makes it clear that other ladies were on guard against being "badly" tanned, with their umbrellas pressed into service as parasols. As usual, the beach is far more crowded than the water.

The famed English Bay bathing house (men only) is visible above the black-clad woman on the right.

Just visible on the right edge of the photo is a young photographer, in a jaunty white hat, with a tripod–mounted camera. One wonders if this is Timms himself, making a cameo appearance in his own photograph. He would have been in his early 30s at the time. It's fun to speculate whether one of the city's most celebrated photographers might have immortalized himself here.

Philip Timms moved to Vancouver from Toronto in 1898, at age 24, and began a picture framing business. He also began immediately to photograph street scenes in his new home. With his photographic equipment strapped to his back, Timms and his bicycle bouncing along the city's rough streets was a familiar sight. He retired in 1968 after 70 years as a commercial photographer, but was still taking photographs into his nineties. He died August 8th, 1973 at 98.

No person shall bathe or swim in the waters of Burrard Inlet or English Bay within the City limits between the hours of 6 o'clock in the forenoon and 8 o'clock in the evening without a bathing dress covering the body from the neck to the knees, and any person wearing such proper bathing dress may bathe at any time in the waters of Burrard Inlet or English Bay within the City limits.

From By-law number 135, 17 March 1892

OUR BATHING BEACH

VANCOUVER. B.C.

TIMMS

View of English Bay shoreline looking east from near Park Lane, 1898. Stuart Thompson / City of Vancouver Archives / BE P90 N45

The English Bay of a century ago has been completely transformed. Where in 1898 lofty trees once marked where Gilford Street met the waters of the Bay, now lofty apartment buildings stand in their place. The "English Bay Club" (for men only), the waterchute, Simpson's boat house; all are now gone. More affluent Vancouverites had summer cottages on the beach, like those just to the left of the tall trees. A more modest budget led some to camp out in big and often elaborately furnished tents. Can you spot the tents on the far shoreline?

Our hunch is that the small group huddled around that Squamish canoe are not among those more affluent citizens. These folks would have made their way to this spot, near the south end of Denman, along a narrow plank walk, taking care not to step into the "wet muskeg of black loam" that was Denman Street of the day. That "muskeg" was fertile ground for a bountiful crop of skunk cabbage. No wonder everyone looks so solemn!

English Bay Beach, Squamish canoe and camper's cottages, C.1895.
City of Vancouver Archives / BE P69B N37B

View of English Bay shoreline looking east from near Park Lane, 2000.

JOE FORTES

The archival caption on this photograph says it best: "The beloved Joe Fortes, his cottage, and his flowers... Moved to this bank above the sandy beach in 1905, and occupied by faithful beach guard until his death in 1922. His memorial fountain stands in Alexandra Park." C.1910 City of Vancouver Archives / BU P111 N111

He came to Vancouver in 1885, aged about 20, in the crew of the *Robert Kerr*, but after a look around jumped ship to stay. His name was Seraphim Fortes, but everyone called him Joe. An award-winning swimmer, Joe and some friends "discovered" English Bay and began to swim there. Soon, this kindly Barbados-born man (who had a job as a bartender at the Sunnyside Hotel in Gastown) began to teach locals how to swim. He was terrifically good at it, and the city made him its official lifeguard. He taught thousands of kids to swim (if you'd been one of them, you would be familiar with his gentle voice saying "Kick yo' feet, chile, kick yo' feet"), and he was credited over the years with saving more than 100 people from drowning. Joe lived alone in a tiny ivy-covered cottage on the beach. When he died in February, 1922 the entire city went into mourning.

"Our friend 'Joe'", demonstrating his diving form, 1906. We must assume the writing on the photo is that of Timms, the photographer, and reflects the affection Vancouverites held for the city's illustrious life guard and swimming teacher.
Philip Timms / Vancouver Public Library / 005469

Here we can almost hear Joe telling the girl to "relax", that "there's nothing to be afraid of", Vancouver Public Library / 009436

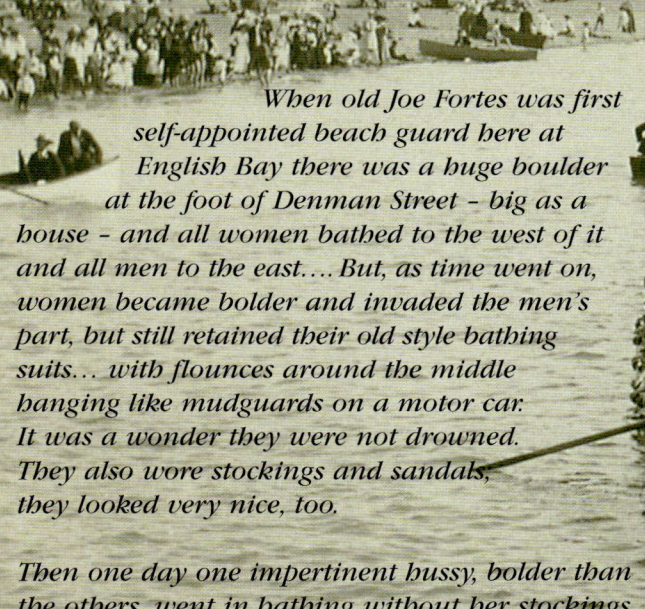

When old Joe Fortes was first self-appointed beach guard here at English Bay there was a huge boulder at the foot of Denman Street - big as a house - and all women bathed to the west of it and all men to the east…. But, as time went on, women became bolder and invaded the men's part, but still retained their old style bathing suits… with flounces around the middle hanging like mudguards on a motor car. It was a wonder they were not drowned. They also wore stockings and sandals, they looked very nice, too.

Then one day one impertinent hussy, bolder than the others, went in bathing without her stockings. She was a sight to behold—she was bare naked right up to her knees. The Women's Christian Temperance Union wrote to the press about it and what they wrote about the bold woman was published in the newspapers. She sued the C.C.T.U for libel. The case went to court and she got damages. From Major J.S. Matthews, "The Great English Bay Scandal", Early Vancouver, volume 7, page 154

This wonderful photo above, taken about 1907, shows a big crowd of people in a long line of rowboats, and an even bigger crowd on the shore, waiting for the boat races to begin on English Bay. One wonders: did we dress formally for EVERYTHING back then?
Philip Timms / Vancouver Public Library / 005462

Starting line for Race Day, 1907. Philip Timms / Vancouver Public Library / 005458

RACE DAY 1930

Brithung Beach . English Bay Vancouver B.C.

It's more than 20 years after the photographs on the preceding page, and Vancouverites are still thrilling to English Bay boat races. But now the Great Depression has started, and the races have become a welcome but all-too-brief diversion from the financial hard times. Another pleasant diversion: Tetley's Tea. Note the big sign.

Almost 75 years have elapsed and we see that the mountains on the north shore, along with the Sylvia Hotel (top right in the old photo – can you find it in the contemporary version?) are in the same place in both photos. Happily, the gazebo - replaced by a faithful recreation - also anchors this scene to the past. But the trees have grown so large all we can see of the gazebo now is the Canadian flag atop it.

National Air Photo Library / BA-12-7

National Air Photo Library / A2605-20

Flying was still a rarity in 1923, but thankfully someone was up there to record this scene of a practically unrecognizable West End in the top photo. The brand-new Marine Building gleams in the distance in the 1930 shot above of English Bay and beyond.

Historian Ed Starkins reminds us that until 1958 the tallest building in the West End was the eight-storey Sylvia Hotel at 1154 Gilford Street. That's it down there on the near shore, just to the right of the now-vanished English Bay Pier. This famous old hotel, built in 1912 and once the site of a famous eighth-floor restaurant ('Dine in the Sky!'), was named by owner Abraham Goldstein for his 12-year-old daughter. The Sylvia actually began as an up-market apartment building, but during the Great Depression became a low-cost hotel for merchant seamen. After the war the glamour returned. The Sylvia is just two blocks from Stanley Park. Over the decades the sturdy old building has become covered in deep green Virginia Creeper ivy . . . planted years ago by a woman tenant! (By the way, Sylvia Goldstein, born March 1, 1900 celebrated her 100th birthday March 1, 2000.)

Morning view north over English Bay Beach to Coal Harbour and central business district, 2001. The low tide reveals stone pilings marking the site of the famous English Bay pier.

Aerial view of the west end, 1925. National Air Photo Library / A2605 513

Aerial view of West End near Lost Lagoon, 2001.

THE WEST END

Afternoon view north over English Bay Beach to the West End's apartment jungle and the central business district, 2001.

The West End today is the most densely populated chunk of British Columbia. Just under 40,000 people are crammed into this lively peninsula, most of them in high-rise apartment blocks that command superb views of English Bay with its boats and ships on one side, and the north shore mountains on the other. Couples stroll hand in hand, Frisbees are thrown, joggers trot by, dogs are walked, tourist buses glide slowly along, browsers haunt the hundreds of shops, diners sit at sidewalk cafes looking at you looking at them, readers pass in and out of the Joe Fortes branch of the library . . . the West End is a people-watcher's paradise. And as the sun sets behind the "sails" of Canada Place in the distance, the lights of the West End blink on and night life begins. Small cafes dot the streets, offering Chinese, Japanese, Thai, Vietnamese, French, Philippine, Mexican, and occasionally even western cuisine!

More than half the population of the West End is under 40, many are transient, and many are college age, so it's lively, noisy and colorful… and would be completely unrecognizable to the Three Greenhorns!

160

View of the West End from the Burrard Street Bridge, 2001.

Tall apartment buildings, of ten storeys or more, will start rising over English Bay within the next five years,. They will mark the second stage of an architectural revolution unique in Vancouver, and so far peculiar to the West End. The first stage is well under way. It has already changed the area west of Denman. It involves the building of modern, steel-and-concrete apartment blocks rising from three to six storeys... The apartment house, once associated with cramped quarters, tenement conditions and a general lowering of residential standards, is now a symbol of rejuvenation.

D'arcy Marsh, "West End Starts Unique Comeback", The Vancouver Sun, 30 March 1958

View of the West End from Burrard Street Bridge, C.1960 Vancouver Public Library / 008919

The second and third Hotels Vancouver provide a backdrop to this 1931 West End panorama, taken from the roof of an apartment building at the corner of Bute and Comox. Vancouver Public Library / 004259

During the 1930s the West End enjoyed a reputation as a "congenial, relaxed and affordable neighborhood". David Savage, a News Herald reporter, lived in the Buchan Hotel at 1906 Haro, paying $40 a month for a large room with maid service and three meals a day. "The West End was a gracious place of beautiful old houses and mellow gardens," Savage wrote. "It was a place for the very young, starting out at very low wages, and the very old, surviving on often very small pensions. Both wanted something cheap, and the West End was cheap."

View to the northeast from the same apartment building as in the photograph at left in 2001. The Hotel Vancouver is just visible if you look closely while it–along with the still operating second Hotel Vancouver–dominate the 1931 skyline. Only two other buildings survive today from the old image. Both apartments, they are the Washington Court at 998 Thurlow and the Caroline Court at 1058 Nelson. Can you find them in both photos?

A contemporary view of the Rogers Mansion in its modern incarnation as Romano's Macaroni Grill.

A couple posing with a thoroughbred horse in front of Gabriola, the B.T. Rogers mansion on Davie Street, C.1900. Vancouver Public Library / 007276

ROGERS HOUSE

At the northwest corner of Davie and Nicola is what has been described as the most lavish private home ever constructed in Vancouver. Named Gabriola by its owner, sugar magnate Benjamin Tingley Rogers, the mansion had its housewarming July 23, 1901 and immediately became a West End landmark. Gabriola is still there today, occupied a century later by Romano's Macaroni Grill, an upscale restaurant.

'Gabriola', B.T. Rogers mansion on Davie, C.1905. Vancouver Public Library

The buggy was disappearing, the motor car was coming; distances were less formidable an obstacle than formerly. The verandah was still a necessity, but rapidly nearing its end, and soon to shrink into a mere porch. The broad verandah, the scene so long of evening parties, of Sunday afternoon gatherings, of sunshine and fresh air in the summer days was about to disappear. The Ford motor car killed it.

from J.S. Matthews, Early Vancouver, volume 1, number 104.

Classic verandah of the Barclay Manor, a resource centre for seniors on Barclay Street.

It is not easy to look back on conditions of 100 years ago because there are so many matters which now enter into daily life as necessities that it is almost impossible to conceive of their absence. First, perhaps, of all is the railroad-but 25 years of the century had passed before there was a single mile of railroad in the world. To-day there are over 450,000 miles. Reverse, for a moment the wheels of progress and run back for a hundred years and what are the experiences. Many and many a mile stone of progress is passed before the journey has proceeded far. The telephone, phonograph and graphophone quickly disappear. Electric railways are lost and electric lights have gone out. The telegraph disappears. The sewing machine, reaper and thrasher have passed away, and so also have all India rubber goods. No longer are there photographs, lithographs, or cameras. The printing press dwindles rapidly in size until it becomes a clumsy hand machine. Planing and woodworking machinery go. There are no gas engines, no passenger elevators, no asphalt pavements, no steam fire-engines…no celluloid articles, no wire fences, no time-locks for safes, no self-binders or harvesters… no cash registers or cash carriers, no great suspension bridges, no canals of any size, no magazine guns, no type-setting machines, no typewriters. All pasteurizing or knowledge of disease germs and microbes disappears. Sanitary plumbing is unknown and of antiseptics or anesthetics there are none. Water gas, soda water, air brakes, coal tar dyes, dynamos, steamships. Bessemer steel with its wonderful developments, dynamite, gun cotton, aluminum ware, ocean cables, enameled iron ware, storage batteries, roller mills, knitting machines, tin can machines, artesian wells, lucifer matches, artificial limbs, nail machines, Xray apparatus, machines for woolen and cotton manufacture-all have disappeared.*

From "The Wonderful Century", The Vancouver Daily Province,
15 December 1900.

TOP: View west along Georgia from Thurlow, C.1900. Vancouver Public Library / 000033

CENTRE: View west along Georgia from Thurlow, 2001.

BOTTOM: View west along Georgia from the first Hotel Vancouver, 1907. Philip Timms / Vancouver Public Library / 007703

The entire history of automobiles, airplanes, antibiotics, oral contraception, nuclear energy, computers, plastics, satellites and xerography is encompassed by the span of a single human life.

David Suzuki, scientist and broadcaster.

View west along Georgia from Richards, 1933. Vancouver Public Library / 005430

COAL HARBOUR

Sunrise view to the east over Coal Harbour from the Seawall in Stanley Park.

Coal Harbour from causeway, 1935 Leonard Frank / Vancouver Public Library / 006340

While HMS *Plumper*, Capt. George Richards in command, was exploring the waters of Burrard Inlet in 1859 Francis Brockton, the ship's chief engineer, discovered coal on the south shore. That inspired Richards to name that part of the inlet Coal Harbour. (You see it above as it was in 1935.) The coal later proved to be a small seam, and of only average quality, but it nonetheless changed the history of the area: a lump of the coal was displayed in a shop window in New Westminster and that attracted the notice of passerby John Morton, a recent arrival from England. Morton was a potter, and he knew that where there was coal there was often also clay. Morton talked with his cousin, Samuel Brighouse, and friend William Hailstone, and the three men pooled resources to buy 500 acres of the surrounding forest. They paid $1.01 per acre, high for the time. That earned them the derisive nickname, the "Three Greenhorns."

For a time the nickname seemed appropriate. There was clay there, but not good enough for pottery, so the men began to make bricks. That didn't work out either.

But having all that land proved to be a bonanza. Morton, especially, did very well as a result of his investment. At his death in 1912 he left an estate of $700,000, equivalent to several million dollars today. Their 500 acres is now the West End of Vancouver.

The ghoulishly named Deadman or Deadman's Island, off Stanley Park, was where early native people placed their dead. The few residents shown in this 1886 photo below were forced off when the Park was created. Even in 1904 Coal Harbour was home to people living on the water (right). The two boating images on the opposite page (center and far right) reflect proper, turn-of-the-century attire for an afternoon on the water.

National Archives of Canada / PA-

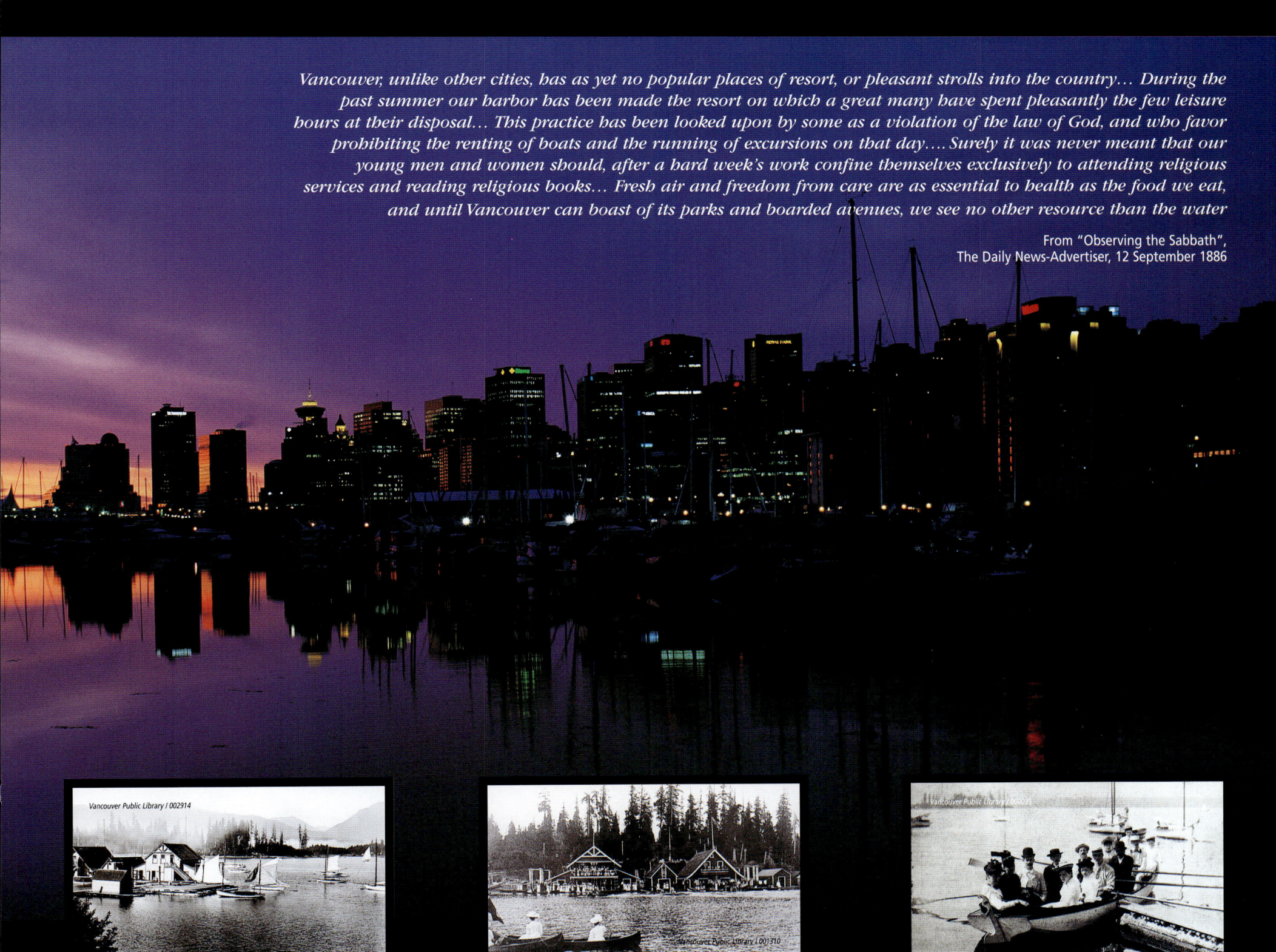

Vancouver, unlike other cities, has as yet no popular places of resort, or pleasant strolls into the country… During the past summer our harbor has been made the resort on which a great many have spent pleasantly the few leisure hours at their disposal… This practice has been looked upon by some as a violation of the law of God, and who favor prohibiting the renting of boats and the running of excursions on that day…. Surely it was never meant that our young men and women should, after a hard week's work confine themselves exclusively to attending religious services and reading religious books… Fresh air and freedom from care are as essential to health as the food we eat, and until Vancouver can boast of its parks and boarded avenues, we see no other resource than the water

From "Observing the Sabbath",
The Daily News-Advertiser, 12 September 1886

STANLEY PARK

Entrance to Stanley Park, 2001

Once upon a time this thousand acres of raw forest was a military reserve, meant to protect the entrance to Vancouver's harbour from possible American invasion. When that threat passed, the little city asked to lease the forest from the federal government for $1 a year. That's how we got Stanley Park, one of the world's great city parks.

If it had been opened a little earlier in 1888, we might be calling it Lansdowne Park. If it had opened five years later, it might have been Aberdeen Park. But the Governor General of Canada when the park was dedicated was Frederick Arthur Stanley, Baron Stanley of Preston, and so "Stanley Park" it was. He'd been sworn in June 11, 1888 and the park was officially dedicated in his name on September 27. (He also gave us the Stanley Cup.)

Entrance to Stanley Park, 1898 Vancouver Public Library / 013496

Paths were created through the new park, a little "zoo" began (it was a bear tied to a tree), refreshment stands opened, and a million squirrels and ducks gorged on bread and other goodies brought by locals. Some of the hardier of those 1905 strollers (above) might intend to walk around the perimeter of the entire park, a nine-kilometre stroll. By 1927 a streetcar line (below) was bringing people from distant points along Georgia Street to the park, where they alighted at Lost Lagoon. From its opening more than 100 years ago, Stanley Park has been Vancouver's major attraction.

Family Portrait, 2nd Beach, July 1st, 1904. Philip Timms / Vancouver Public Library / 007236

No television, no radio, no hand-held electronic games, no Pokemon, no skateboards or in-line skates or scooters…just sun and sand, family and friends.

We count 22 people on this crowded little patch of Stanley Park's Second Beach (can you spot them all?), but there's no food, so it isn't a picnic. All three adults are women; are they teachers, governesses, very fertile mothers? We don't know. We do know that Second Beach (so named because it's the next stretch of sand to the north of the beach at English Bay) was a popular spot for Sunday afternoon sunning . . . even if there's not a bathing suit in sight in this picture taken about 1906. These kids would enjoy Second Beach today, with its seaside pool and waterslides. But, just like the two young girls in the small photo at left, children can also find the simple pleasures like a stick in the sand a focus for play.

Could those two little girls in front be twins? And could that big log still be on the beach today, a century later, still providing bountiful seating for beach visitors?

173

Lost Lagoon, C.1866 (may be earliest photo of Vancouver) Frederick Dally / Vancouver Public Library / 004207

LOST LAGOON

The native poet Pauline Johnson (1862-1913) named this famous spot near the entrance of what is now Stanley Park. She wrote of paddling her canoe to the lagoon one day to discover that when the tide went out its calm, reflective waters completely disappeared. With the development of the park, the lagoon was enclosed and Lost Lagoon, though it retains that name, is lost no more. (Those tumbledown shacks are, however.)

The serenity of Lost Lagoon inspired one of her most well-known poems, which begins:

It is dusk on the Lost Lagoon,
And we two dreaming the dusk away,
Beneath the drift of a twilight grey,
Beneath the drowse of an ending day,
And the curve of a golden moon.

"Coal Harbor at high tide covers an area of 51 acres. At low tide, or the greater part of the time it may be 10 acres. The rest is mud. What I want is a permanent sheet of water artistically treated and 35 acres in extent… In the centre of this lake I want to see a great sculptured didactic monument. Round this monumental lake … the people should be provided with a wide flagged path where they may perambulate free from quick moving traffic…"

From an address to the Canadian Club luncheon by Thomas H. Mawson, secretary of the British Institute of Art as reported in the Daily News-Advertiser, 28 March 1912, under the headline ' Beautification of Coal Harbor'.

Aerial view of Lost Lagoon and high rises of the West End that border on Stanley Park.

High-rise apartments of the West End reflected in the tranquil waters of early-morning Lost Lagoon.

Clockwise from the top; Coal Harbour at first light on a day that could go either way, English Bay sunset, Burrard Inlet, Prospect Point Lighthouse from Lions Gate Bridge, replica figurehead from SS Empress of Japan and low tide near Brockton Point.

SEAWALL PROMENADE

If there was to be a book or film on the World's Greatest Walks the 9 kilometre Seawall encircling Stanley Park would be the cover feature or lead by which all others would be judged. We throw out superlatives like magnificent, grand, awe inspiring, spectacular and beautiful much too freely in our daily conversation so that when we really need one, they are all diluted by over use. A complete circuit yields vistas of the downtown core, Burrard Inlet, the North Shore, Georgia Strait, English Bay, Kitsilano and English Bay. To spend a sunny day exploring this glorious promenade is – by itself - worth a flight from anywhere in the world.

Queen Brothers Stanley Park Stables on the south side of Georgia between Granville and Seymour occupied the site of today's Scotia Tower. City of Vancouver Archives / BU P84 N131

The tradition of horse-drawn conveyances in the Park is carried on today by Gerry O'Neil pictured at right and his AAA Horse & Carriage in Stanley Park Ltd.

Gerry O'Neil posing with one of his Stanley Park rigs in front of the Scotia Tower on Georgia. This is the same location as we see in the old photo of Stanley Park Stables.

The number of people photographed within Stanley Park's famous Hollow Tree in the more than 115 years of the park's existence is anyone's guess--it's certainly many hundreds of thousands. From the moment horse-drawn carriages could navigate the park's early roads people began to arrive for pictures in this scenic spot. Then when the automobile arrived local folk used them to bring their families and visiting friends and relatives to pose here. In fact, the very first car to arrive in Vancouver (it was 1899 and the car was a Stanley Steamer) puffed and burped its way into the park for the traditional picture. There was even a brief period when some enterprising young fellow -likely just as a gag--set up a bar in the tree's hollow and sold drinks to thirsty passers by! People have had pictures taken of themselves to set into the family album beside pictures taken decades earlier of their grandparents in this same famous tree.

One great difference in those pictures is readily apparent: in the old days the tree kept going up. Today, because of its age, it exists only as a tall stump and even that is held together with metal straps.

A few steps away from the Hollow Tree strollers find the "National Geographic Tree," so named because that magazine named it the world's largest red cedar, at almost 30 metres (100 feet) around. (Canada's tallest big leaf maple and tallest red alder both also grow within the park)

There are many, many other botanical and scenic wonders along Stanley Park's 35 kilometres of forested trails.

The Hollow Tree, despite its deteriorating condition, continues to star in thousands of family albums. And perhaps realizing its time is limited, the old stump has taken on the duties of 'nurse tree' to another cedar growing right out of her own base on the right.

Hollow Tree, C.1900 Philip Timms / Vancouver Public Library / 005487

Cars at Parks Board Shelter, Prospect Point, 1905 Philip Timms / Vancouver Public Library / 005487

A 1904 automobile club excursion in Stanley Park Vancouver Public Library / 004203

Parks Board Shelter, Prospect Point, 1900 Note partially thatched roof and forest on north shore.
Philip Timms / Vancouver Public Library / 008286

PROSPECT POINT

Hmm. Three ladies, two men. Is it possible there's a third gentleman, and he's taking the picture? Cyclists would have found Stanley Park a great adventure, with scenic treasures on every side. But that little thatched gazebo has seen better days! Note the prospect visible from the Prospect Point (64 metres above sea level) of 1900: the north shore is a vast tract of trees. The 1901 census showed there were 365 people living in North Vancouver, but they were all huddled to the west of this view.

If the gazebo visible in the picture above (right) is the same one, then things have improved in the five years from the 1900 of the bicyclists to the 1905 of the motorists. We took to the car quickly in Vancouver and, in fact, in 1904 the city's first auto dealership was opened by brothers Frank and Fred Begg. The first gasoline-powered car was bought that year by industrialist John Hendry, after whom the East End's John Hendry Park is named, and a clever fellow named Harry Hooper was running a taxi service, the first in the city.

The car began changing things quickly: roads had to be paved, bridges would be designed to accommodate the new phenomenon, new rules of the road would have to be imposed… but there was still time for fun, and for the forming of auto clubs. Such a club may very well be what's parading by in that 1904 picture, watched enviously by a boy off to the side who won't have his hands on a steering wheel for a few years yet. On Labour Day in 1905 the first auto club race was held around Stanley Park's perimeter road. Eleven cars started, but only five finished. An oddity: all five were Oldsmobiles. A great advertisement for them!

Today, cars and their passengers still descend on Prospect Point, but one thing is very different: those 1904 motorists wouldn't have known what a parking meter was. Alas, we do today… even in Stanley Park.

Aerial view of Prospect Point.

Visitors and locals alike enjoy the spectacular views from Prospect Point.

PROSPECT POINT

Alex in Wonderland is the Vancouver Aquarium's title for their wonderful image of the momentary connection between boy and beluga whale. Exhibit themes include the Canadian Arctic, Canada's rugged West Coast, tropical Amazon and the coral reefs of the South Pacific.

Jeff Vinnick / Vancouver Aquarium Marine Science Centre

Aerial view looking south over Brockton Point, Coal Harbour, and the West End to Kitsilano and English Bay. The Aquarium is hidden in the wooded area to the right, near the entrance to the Park.

Totem Pole Display, 1927 Vancouver Public Library i 004600

Totem Pole Display, 2001

TOTEMS

Totem Pole Display, 1936 Vancouver Public Library / 004604

They have been called the world's most viewed totem poles: some eight million people visit Stanley Park every year, and it would be difficult to tour the park and not see (and photograph) these striking attractions near Brockton Point. These poles at Stanley Park are genuine, carved and painted by native craftsmen . . . but it must be said their style does not represent the local Salish people. These spectacular totems were carved by Haida and Kwakiutl people from further up the coast.

It was getting easier for people to get around in Vancouver in 1927 (top picture, left). In fact, two-car streetcars were introduced that year, an indication of the growth in population and increased reliance on public transit. It's only in relatively recent times that everyone seems to have a car.

Low man on the totem pole? Don't believe it! The lowest part of the pole is the one looked at most closely, and so the chief carver of the group will personally carve the bottom three or four metres of the pole. The higher, less clearly seen portions are given to less experienced apprentices to carve. These family or clan emblems (think of them as akin to crests or coats of arms) often tell a story, and often the most important elements or people in that story are at the bottom of the pole. The next time you pass by one of these totem poles, try to figure out the story!

The 1936 photo (bottom right) shows how, as the population of Vancouver increased, the park became neater.

One thing is constant: our continuing fascination with these unique symbols of family pride and tradition.

The Prospect Point lighthouse (lower left) went into operation October 1, 1898, so it's still fairly new in this 1905 photo. Lighthouses were manned back then, so it's not unlikely that the lighthouse keeper might exchange a wave with passengers crowding the rails aboard the liners entering and leaving the harbour. (Incidentally, the official description of Vancouver's boundaries in the city's charter uses the light at Prospect Point as the starting point.) That's a radio facility at the top of the hill above the lighthouse.

BROCKTON POINT

View west through 1st Narrows with Prospect Point Lighthouse and radio facility, C.1905
Vancouver Public Library / 003060

Brockton Point bathed in the soft light of a spring sunrise.

Princess Victoria passing Brockton Point Light, C.1908. Philip Timms / Vancouver Public Library / 002902

Lighthouses were popping up all over the continent's seaboards in the late 1800s as commercial ships and passenger liners began to increase in numbers. There has been a light at Brockton Point (lower right) at the eastern tip of Stanley Park since September of 1890. The point was named for Francis Brockton, chief engineer of HMS *Plumper* (and the man, remember, who in 1859 discovered the coal that gave Coal Harbour its name.)

The Brockton Point Lighthouse seen today by strollers and joggers along the Stanley Park Seawall is not the one shown here. The improved structure you see today was built in 1915. The next time you go by, try to spot the arch at the bottom of the structure--which was designed by early Vancouver landscape architect Thomas Mawson. The arch is all that remains of what was originally intended to be part of a shelter for lifeboats, but treacherous currents at the point made that impractical. Both lighthouses were automated in 1926.

Traffic in 1905—although there was precious little of it—was enjoined to "Keep Left," but we're not sure whether these two ladies and their pram are obeying that rule. We do know that this magnificent Philip Timms photograph captures the quiet splendor of Stanley Park a century ago. Philip Timms / Vancouver Public Library / 007286

Boathouse in Stanley Park

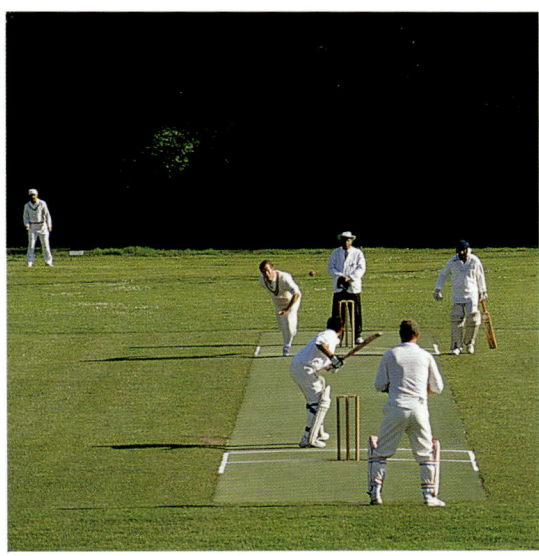

Building a thirst on the Cricket Pitch

Quenching a Cricket thirst at Brockton Clubhouse.

Nature's sculpture

Seawall Promenade on Burrard Inlet

Girl in Wet Suit sculpture, by Elek Imredy

Empress of Japan sailing away through the First Narrows, 1901. Note the heavily forested north shore of a century ago. Today this area at the mouth of the Capilano River encompasses Ambleside park, Park Royal Shopping Centre and a flourishing West Vancouver. Vancouver Public Library / 002980

Off to Yokohama! Canadian Pacific's *Empress of Japan* is seen here about 1901 steaming through the First Narrows en route to the East. The *'Japan'* was one of the fastest passenger liners in the world at the time, making just under 19 knots. Oddly, although quite good statistics are available for the number of people coming *in* to Canada aboard the *Empresses*, we know virtually nothing about how many people left aboard them!

That modern P&O liner leaving for Alaska carries more than 2,000 passengers. There are about 300 sailings to and from Alaska before the season ends in October. And the cruise business in total? More than 800,000 cruise vacationers sail out of Vancouver in a typical year.

We think we can make an educated guess about what some of those 1901 passengers might say about their counterparts 100 years later: "You're going to Alaska for a *vacation*?"

P&O's Radiance of the Seas bound for Alaska, off Prospect Point.

THE EMPRESSES

For 50 years, from 1891 to 1941, the handsome white steamers of Canadian Pacific's Empress line provided passenger, freight and mail service between Vancouver and the Orient. The first three to be built at Barrow-in-Furness on the west coast of England–*the Empress of India, Empress of Japan* and *Empress of China*–cost more than $1 million each, an immense cost for the time. Compared to the giant cruise ships of today, they were tiny (a gross tonnage of 5,940, compared to well over 100,000 for today's largest), but they were the last word in luxury and speed for the time. By 1897 the Empresses, facing heavy competition, were carrying 60 per cent of all first-class Pacific travel.

The photograph at right, taken about 1910, shows one of these handsome ships readying to leave Vancouver's port. (When she arrived, by the way, she would have brought in–besides hundreds of passengers–valuable cargos of silk and tea. As an example in just one 40-day period the Empresses brought in four silk cargoes valued at $6 million.) Besides the passengers she will take away, she carries mail and will have flour and cotton goods in her cargo. For years, those were the two big export items. Most of the flour went to China and Australia. (At about the time of this photograph Vancouver longshoremen struck for higher pay. They wanted 35 cents per hour for day work and 40 cents per hour for night work. They got it.)

The photo on the opposite page shows the *Empress of India* docked at the CP Pier April 28, 1891. This is her first visit to Vancouver, and that crowd has come down to see her. In the six years the city has existed, the population has grown to nearly 14,000. This new ship (which, by the way, may include in her cargo opium, legal at the time) is just another indication that in 1901 Vancouver is booming. By 1910 the Vancouver Opera House has opened on Granville Street, famed actress Sarah Bernhardt appears there in *Fedora*, Edison's amazing gramophone arrives, the Interurban whisks people to New Westminster (which has just got electric street lights), and H.O. Bell-Irving forms the Anglo-British Columbia Packing Co., soon to become the world's largest producer of canned salmon.

Yes, things are going splendidly. Just one question: why doesn't that fellow in the foreground in the picture above buy a bigger hat?

"THE PARTING AT THE DOCK"   VANCOUVER, B.C. TIMMS

Departure of an Empress, C.1910.   Vancouver Public Library / 002970

Empress of India arriving at CPR Pier, 1891. Vancouver Public Library / 002970

The excitement of arriving and departing cruise ships today is hidden in the enclosed lounges that handle passengers using Canada Place.

Aerial view of Vancouver harbour with Empress of Canada docked at CPR pier, 1930. National Air Photo Library / A 2605 25

VANCOUVER HARBOUR

After the first three, the Empresses got larger, as you can see above in this striking 1930 aerial photograph of the harbour. That's *the Empress of Canada* (launched August 17, 1920) docked at the CPR pier. The *Canada*--at 653 feet the longest ship to cross the Pacific to that time--was a great advance on her predecessors: she was more luxurious, had a full extra deck, had amenities like elevators and swimming pools. One of her three funnels was a dummy, added for aesthetic reasons. A year after this picture was taken, the Canada set a speed record--21.78 knots--for the run between Yokohama and Honolulu.

Aerial view of cruise ship docked at Canada Place, 2001.

View of Coal Harbour from Deadman Island, 1935. The Empress of Japan can just be seen at the CPR pier while the Marine Building and the new Hotel Vancouver tower over the skyline. Vancouver Public Library / 006000

Five years later, a 1935 view of the harbour (above) taken from Deadman's Island shows *the Empress of Japan II* in dock. The five-year-old Marine Building and the unfinished Hotel Vancouver dominate the skyline. The *Japan II*, launched December 17, 1929, was an advance over the *Canada*: 13 feet longer, six feet wider, more luxurious, even faster and much less expensive to operate. Unfortunately, the world-wide depression impacted badly on both passenger and cargo numbers for the *Empress* line and the service would end in a few years. The emergence of Alaska as a cruise destination revived Vancouver as a port of embarkation for vacationers seeking this northern experience.

Early morning arrival of cruise ship moving silently toward her birth at Canada Place.

Panoramic view of the Harbour from the first Hotel Vancouver, 1891. Vancouver Public Library / 000049(bottom)

When the Empress of India sailed into Vancouver harbour in 1891, the six-year-old city (above) was beginning to find its feet. It had passed New Westminster in population a few years before, now had 13,709 residents to New West's 6,678. By 1911 (below) the city's skyline had undergone an astonishing change. The pace of building was feverish, and walking around town you saw new structures rising on every side. Yet 1911 Vancouver still had its raw side: historian Bruce Macdonald writes that local horses of the day had learned to place their hooves in the cracks between street bricks "to get a better grip."

Panoramic view of the Harbour from North Vancouver, 2001.

Panoramic view of the Harbour from the second Hotel Vancouver, 1923. Vancouver Public Library / 000049(top)

By 1923 (above) the population is more than 130,000. There had been a severe drop in building activity after 1913, but the 1914 opening of the Panama Canal eased the pain: the canal provided a cheaper way to ship out fish, grain and lumber. By the 1920s things were getting back on track--too fast for some! "Vancouver will have no skyscrapers," the Province wrote October 25, 1929, "if the City Council accepts the advice of its Town Planning Commission . . . This morning the commission again endorsed the provision of the city charter which requires all buildings to be within ten storeys in height or 120 feet." By the way, radio waves are zapping around in the picture above. Radio came to Vancouver in 1922 and by '23 there were four stations: CKMO (the first, and still around as CFUN), CFYC, CKWX (also still here) and CHCL.

Panoramic view of the Harbour from North Vancouver, 1911. National Archives of Canada / PA 029849

Aerial view to the west along the busy harbour to Coal Harbour and Stanley Park. Alaska-bound cruise ships are colourful and regular visitors to Canada Place from May to October.

Aerial view east from Lost Lagoon along harbour, 1925. National Air Photo Liabrary / BA 12 35
There is a conspicuous absence of the high-rise apartment and condo towers that characterize the 2000 view below.

This (left) is what an exciting city looks like in the 21st century. Canada Place, under its dazzlingly white sails, seems about to break away from the shoreline and leave for distant lands. An armada of small boats huddles in Coal Harbour, traffic streams through the narrow streets (except in rush hour!), SkyTrain glides into a station to disgorge a horde of office workers, visitors from a dozen other countries emerge from giant, gleaming cruise ships, people step into and out of a thousand shops, hotel guests gaze down on the streets from numberless windows, couriers on bikes swoop and glide between the buildings . . . a city is motion.

The motion was slower in 1925 (above), simply because there were fewer people. In this aerial photograph, taken from above Lost Lagoon more than 75 years ago, and looking over the same area as in the 2001 shot, there are no high-rise apartment buildings, no soaring condo towers. We weren't there, but we bet it was quieter, too.

FERRIES

One day someone is going to write a full-length book about the ferries that served Greater Vancouver. They performed a valuable and reliable service. There are a couple of small books (by Barr and by Burnes) about the early years of the Burrard Inlet service, but they're short of real detail. One remarkable statistic stands out: it's been estimated that the homely little North Vancouver #2 Ferry, in operation from 1905 to 1936, carried 30 million passengers and two million vehicles over its working lifetime!

To the left, holidaying crowds (it's Dominion Day, 1908) alight from streetcars at the foot of Lonsdale to take the ferry over to Vancouver on the south shore. The same area is considerably different about 1890, as seen in the small inset photo on the opposite page. (There was a regularly scheduled ferry service between Vancouver and North Vancouver by 1893.) By 1936, opposite page, the transformation is startling: most passengers now have their own cars, and there are line-ups—a modern-day phenomenon with which we're all too painfully aware.

Captain James Barr, in his little 1969 book *Ferry Across the Harbour,* tells a terrific story about one unusual rider: "Another passenger I recall was a brindle bulldog who travelled by himself over to Vancouver on certain days of the week . . . He was a rather casual, stand-offish sort of dog and paid no attention whatever to his fellow passengers. One day he was seen emerging from a Vancouver butcher shop with a huge bone in his mouth, so we deduced that his periodic trips to Vancouver were for business purposes only. The old dog was a model passenger except in one respect: he never paid a fare!"

The West Vancouver service ended February 8, 1947, the North Vancouver service August 30, 1958, but the SeaBus began June 17, 1977 and is going strong.

View southwards from Esplanade and Lonsdale to Burrard Inlet, C.1908. North Vancouver Museum & Archives / 000496

View southwards from 2nd Street over Lonsdale Quay area to Burrard Inlet, 2001.

View of Terminal at the foot of Main Street for ferries to North Vancouver, 1936.
Vancouver Public Library / 023862

View of Hastings Mill at the foot of Dunlevy Street, C1890.
Vancouver Public Library / 019775

North Vancouver Museum & Archives / 001455

North Vancouver Museum & Archives / 002976

North Vancouver Museum & Archives / 001456

LONSDALE AVE NORTH VAN. BC

North Vancouver Museum & Archives / 003220

This fascinating sequence of photographs shows the foot of Lonsdale on the north shore of Burrard Inlet from 1905 to 1920. Notice in the 1905 photograph (upper left) that there are poles up, but no wires yet attached. A year later (middle left) and not only are there wires— electricity arrived August 15, 1906 after a cable was laid across the Second Narrows—but now there are sidewalks. 1906 brought the telephone, too, to North Vancouver. (But with tongue planted firmly in cheek, we must confess that progress doesn't seem to have affected the man on the bridge in the 1905 picture. He's only halfway across in the 1906 shot!)

The photographers may have stood on the deck of the St. George, a ferry launched in 1905 and renamed North Vancouver Ferry #2 in 1908 after the city took the money-losing service over.

By 1908 (lower left) modern times have arrived . . . with electricity and streetcars. The streetcars were second-hand, it's true, and sometimes prone to ending up in the inlet when things went wrong, but they signified growth. There's something else different in that third photo you can't physically see: North Vancouver City has been created. The city, formed around this very area, broke away from the District in 1907 to become its own entity.

And by 1920 (above) the little city is booming with a population of about 7,600, twice that of the much larger district.

What a lot of information that photograph above gives us: it rewards detailed examination.

View north up Lonsdale from pilot house of Seven Seas Restaurant, 2001.

Cates Tugs, Seven Seas Restaurant and Burrard Dry Dock area of lower Lonsdale from Lonsdale Quay pier, 2001.

View to the northwest at the corner of Lonsdale and Esplanade, 2001

A warm, sunny day in 1904 on The Esplanade in North Vancouver, and that couple seems to be eyeing that Ice Cream sign. We think we know what they want! This long shoreside thoroughfare has been a feature of North Vancouver for a century: Swedish-born Peter Larson built the Hotel North Vancouver on West Esplanade in 1902, and it quickly became a community centre. And 1904 was the year a Maine-born businessman named Charles Cates built a wharf in North Vancouver that served as a transshipment point for goods shipped to the gold-mad Klondike. Cates would later establish his world-famous tugboat firm near the spot pictured above.

Could the little stores shown at left have provided some of the food for the picnic in that fabulous 1906 Philip Timms photograph opposite?

Couple enjoying summer sunshine on Esplanade, 1904. The arachival caption on this photo indicates the address of 106 for the ice cream parlour. That address today is the shop directly above the old photo on the north side of the Esplanade in the contemporary view. Philip Timms / Vancouver Public Library / 005668

Ladies' enjoying picnic lunch in Victoria Park, North Vancouver, 1906. We don't know for certain that it was Victoria Park, but the slope of the land in the background suggests this location. The colour photo at right was taken in Victoria Park and we hope it is related to the trees we see in the 1906 image. Philip Timms / Vancouver Public Library / 007201

203

NORTH VANCOUVER

North Vancouver City, like a lot of communities in Canada and the U.S., had a rough time of it during the Great Depression (its tax base hammered by the loss of industry and its citizens' lack of money), and in 1933 went into receivership. For eleven long years it was run by a commissioner, a one-man government. The top picture shows the city in 1950, just six years after it returned to self-government. The population was about 15,000. By 1965 (the lower picture) the population was about 28,000.

A lot had happened in the interval between these two pictures! The Lions Gate Bridge was sold to the provincial government, which in 1963 dropped the tolls that had been in place for 17 years. The Upper Levels Highway had been completed in 1957, and if you look closely you can see in the distance in the 1965 picture highrise apartment buildings paralleling that busy route. Ferry service to Vancouver had ended August 30, 1958, after years of rapidly plummeting passenger totals (more people buying cars), but the Second Narrows Bridge opened to traffic in 1960. And travellers to Grouse Mountain were bringing income to the city

The little city, born in 1907 and subsisting for many years on logging, now moves ahead fueled by tourism, high technology, a lot of retail business, a share of B.C.'s movie-making prosperity and waterfront industries like shipbuilding and towing. The population of North Vancouver City today is well over 40,000.

Aerial view of Lonsdale area of North Vancouver, 2001.

Aerial view of Lonsdale area of North Vancouver, C.1950 North Vancouver Museum & Archives / 005734A

Aerial view of Lonsdale area of North Vancouver, C.1965 North Vancouver Museum & Archives / 009287

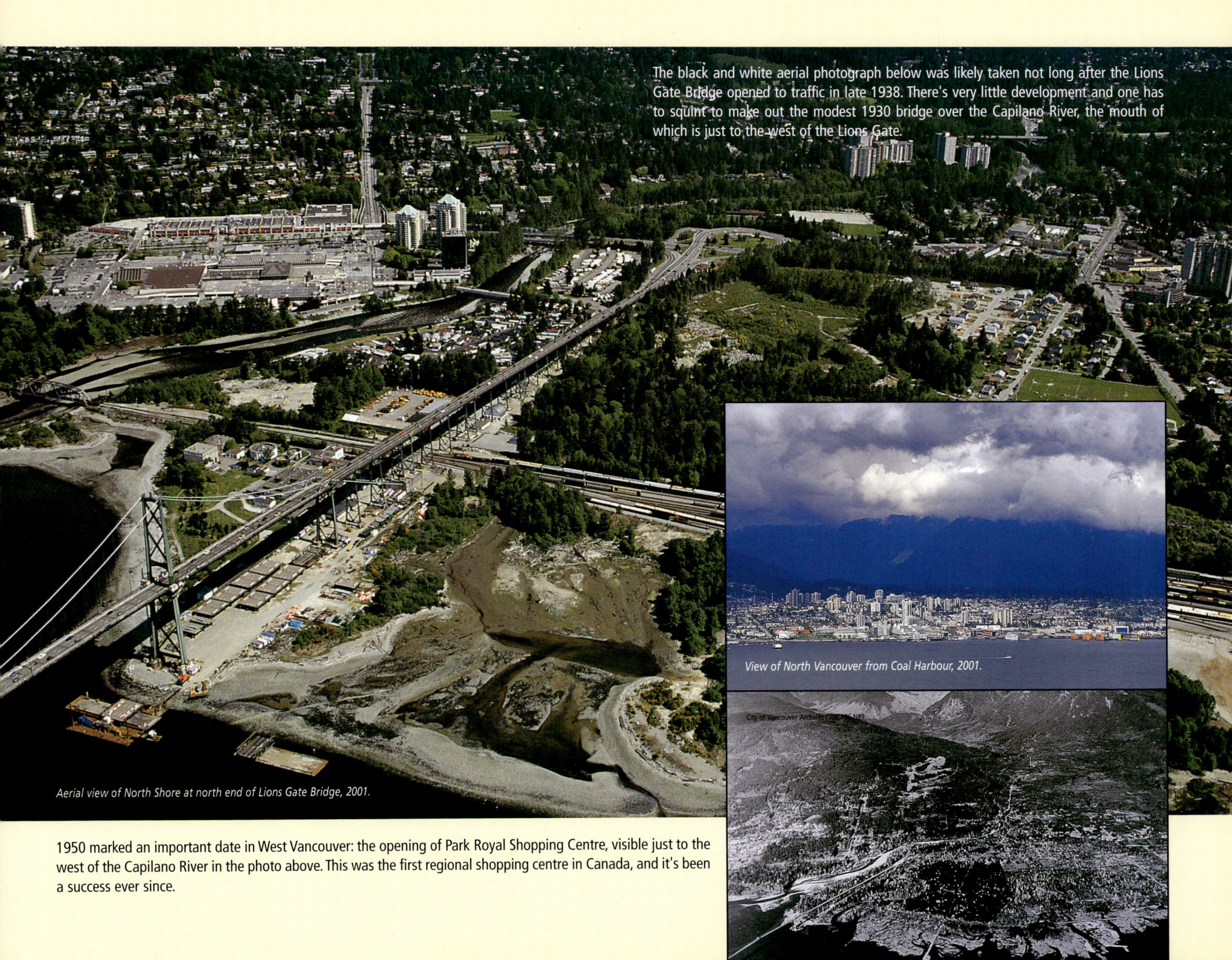

The black and white aerial photograph below was likely taken not long after the Lions Gate Bridge opened to traffic in late 1938. There's very little development and one has to squint to make out the modest 1930 bridge over the Capilano River, the mouth of which is just to the west of the Lions Gate.

View of North Vancouver from Coal Harbour, 2001.

City of Vancouver Archives, AIR P96 N89

Aerial view of North Shore at north end of Lions Gate Bridge, 2001.

1950 marked an important date in West Vancouver: the opening of Park Royal Shopping Centre, visible just to the west of the Capilano River in the photo above. This was the first regional shopping centre in Canada, and it's been a success ever since.

Aerial close-up of Dundarave Pier at low tide, 2001.

View north over West Vancouver's ever popular Dundarave Pier, 1950.
Vancouver Public Library / 081245

WEST VANCOUVER

There was no industry 50 years ago in West Vancouver, and there's no industry today. They don't mind. They want it that way. This 1950 aerial photograph of this most affluent of British Columbia municipalities shows the familiar old Dundarave Pier, built in 1914 to provide access to ferry service from Dundarave to downtown Vancouver. It was never used for ferries, however: the tides were too dangerous! John Lawson's pier in Hollyburn was used instead. But, as you can see opposite, Dundarave Pier became a favorite spot with swimmers and fishermen.

An early resident, Russell Macnaghten, Professor of Greek at the University of British Columbia, named this part of West Van after Dundarave Castle in Scotland, the ancestral home of the Clan Macnaghten. Dundarave, which is supposed to rhyme with "have," is a Gaelic word for a two-oared boat.

View north over West Vancouver's ever popular Dundarave Pier, 2001.

Boinggggg! And off the diving board he goes. You have to look closely to see the airborne boy in mid-dive off the board at Dundarave Pier in this undated photograph. (Their bathing suits point to a pre-1930s date, a time when men, like women, were required to wear tops.) Captured in a single photograph, the golden days of summer and a simpler, slower life style that will never return.

In the background in both pictures is one of the grand old ladies in the local restaurant trade. Open since 1912 (first as a teahouse called the Clachan), known for more than 30 years as Peppi's (1963-94), it's now The Beach House at Dundarave Pier.

View to the beautiful shoreline from the end of Dundarave Pier, 2001. It is possible to stroll along the shoreline almost four kilometres from here, all the way to Ambleside Park at the mouth of the Capilano River.

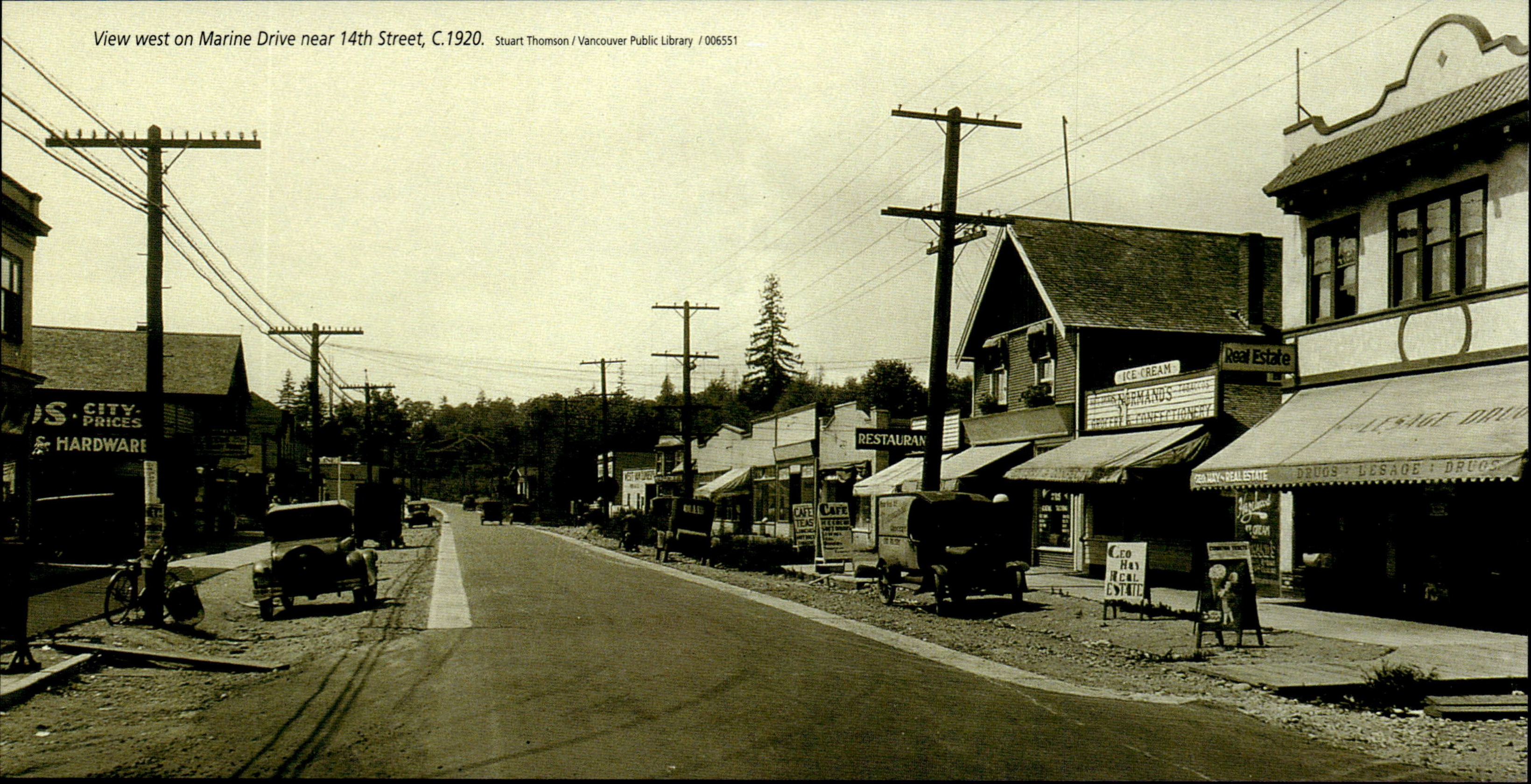

View west on Marine Drive near 14th Street, C.1920. Stuart Thomson / Vancouver Public Library / 006551

Marine Drive is paved in this shot of pre-1922 West Vancouver, but farther up into the slopes of the north shore it wasn't always this modern!

West Van began as a getaway, a summer retreat from the busy haunts of the south shore of Burrard Inlet. It was the opening of the Lions Gate Bridge in 1938, and the development of British Pacific Properties, that forever altered this almost bucolic scene.

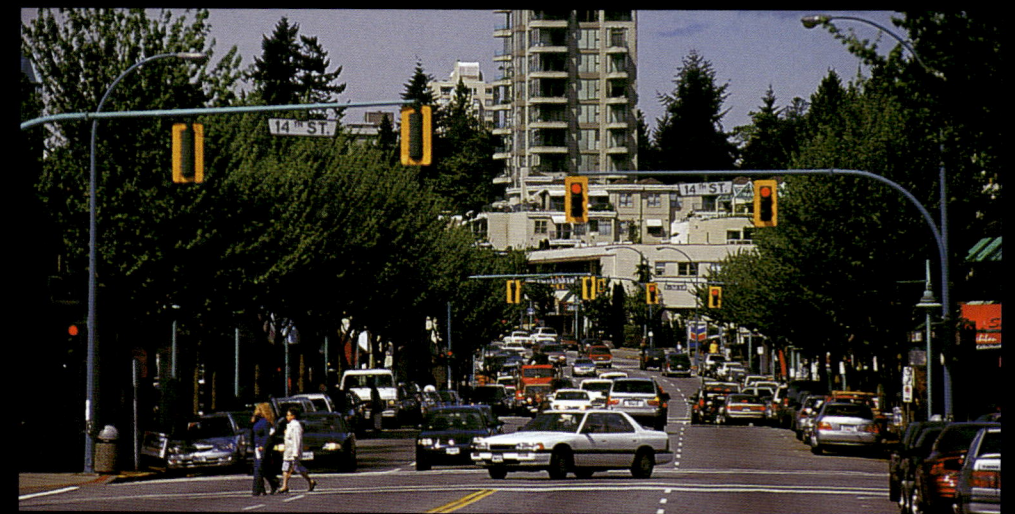

View west on Marine Drive near 14th Street, 2001.

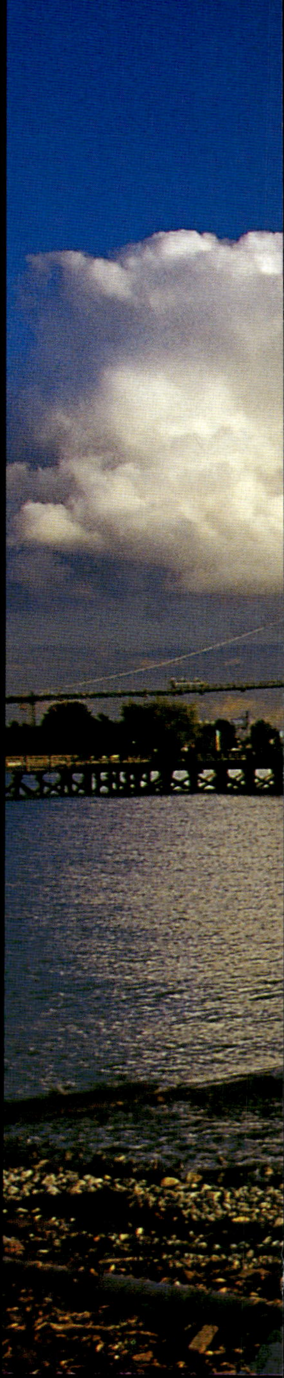

Two couples share the delights of a sunny Sunday on the pier at John Lawson Park.

Just a few short blocks from busy Marine Drive and 14th pictured at left, residents of West Vancouver enjoy the spectacular views of Ambleside and John Lawson parks. Their Sea Wall stretches from Ambleside all the way to Dundarave Park, a distance of about 15 city blocks.

Aerial view to the south over Point Atkinson Lighthouse, 2001.

Ferries from Nanaimo and Bowen Island steaming into Horseshoe Bay, 2001.

Yacht Mou Ping cruising west with the original Point Atkinson lighthouse in the background, C.1906.
Philip Timms / Vancouver Public Library / 007774

The original lighthouse at Point Atkinson went into operation May 1, 1875. It's the stubby little building in the distance past the *Mou Ping* out on a Weekend Cruise. Edwin and Ann Woodward were the first lightkeepers here, and their son James Atkinson Woodward was the first white child born in West Vancouver. Incidentally, the *Mou Ping*, out of the Royal Vancouver Yacht Club, was owned by the sugar magnate B. T. Rogers. Maybe he's aboard her in this 1906 picture… living the sweet life? The present-day lighthouse, erected in 1912, stands tall in spectacular Lighthouse Park.

During World War Two there was a gun emplacement here to help guard the harbor entrance. This patch of land was originally set aside as a timber preserve to provide fuel for the lighthouse and its steam fog alarm. So the 75-hectare park, designated a National Historic Site in 1994, has never been logged, and still has many of its original native trees (including majestic Douglas firs) and plants. More than 60 bird species have been spotted here. A lovely spot to visit, the park is owned by the Ministry of Transport and leased to West Vancouver.

Point Atkinson lighthouse, 2000.

Defiance docked in Deep Cove, 1907.

DEEP COVE

It's only a 20-minute drive from Vancouver, but Deep Cove is in another world: a quiet, friendly, and interesting waterside community. To quote the local historical society, "The first permanent residents in Deep Cove were John and Rhoda Moore and their five children. In 1919 they bought two lots for $15.00 each, cleared the land themselves and survived the first year on wild berries, fish caught in Deep Cove and clams from Roche Point." Some of that informal style is still evident in Deep Cove today. There was a time, though, when a thriving mill here gave work to many locals. The Dollar Mill, named for its owner, Robert Dollar, was in operation from 1917 to 1943. It was a busy, modern mill and shipped lumber all over the world. (Ships carrying that lumber sported a $ on their funnels!) The little community that arose around it became known as Dollar's Town and then Dollarton. Locals like to toodle over to Dollarton on sunny summer days to see what "laid back" really means.

Deep Cove Harbour, 2001.

Cleveland Dam nearing completion, 1955. Look closely at the now dry Capilano riverbed below and you can see the smaller dam is also under construction for the Capilano Salmon Hatchery.

Aerial view of Cleveland Dam, 2001. The Capilano Salmon Hatchery is visible just below the dam.

There are salmon in the river, which is also famous for its suspension bridge and rainforest. The river is turbulent in winter and spring, and that brings in the kayakers–at least, the more adventurous ones! The river subsides in the summer for beginners. Trivia fans will be delighted to learn that the 1936 musical hit movie *Rose Marie*, starring Jeanette MacDonald and Nelson Eddy, was partly filmed along the Capilano!

BRIDGES

Yikes! The Capilano Suspension Bridge--the Lower Mainland's first tourist attraction-- has been scaring people for more than a century. It began when a Scottish-born civil engineer named George Grant Mackay moved to Vancouver in 1888 and bought 6,000 acres of north shore land, through which the Capilano River ran. He built a cabin on the edge of the canyon wall and then, assisted by two local native men and a team of horses, suspended a hemp rope and cedar-plank bridge across the river to his property on the other side. It was 1889.

That scary span, 230 feet above the river, attracted the more adventurous of Mackay's friends and then their friends and Vancouver's first visitor draw was born. (Local native people called it the "laughing bridge" because of the noise it made when wind blew through the canyon.) The bridge has been rebuilt more than once, and today's is very much stronger than the one that that dressed-in-their-Sunday-best party was "enjoying" in 1906. Note the lady in white clinging to her friends on either side.

Today's bridge, the fourth, attracts more than 800,000 visitors a year.

While the bridge has been rebuilt three times since the photograph at left was taken, the attraction and appearance of the bridge and canyon remains largely unchanged nearly 100 years on.

Capilano Canyon Suspension Bridge, 1905. Here, as today, we see the bridge frightens some while intriguing others. Clearly, the woman in white on the right is clinging to the hands of two people while her friend in the center is leaning over the rope hand-rail.
City of Vancouver Archives / BR P59#1 N48#1

The Lion's Gate Bridge spanning the First Narrows, silhouetted by a rising sun. This photo was taken in the Fall of 2000 and the progress of re-building work can be seen approaching the north tower.

Morning commuters jammed up on the Lions Gate Bridge look down in envy at the Alaska-bound cruise ship passengers passing below.

It's 1938 and the First Narrows Bridge (later to be named the Lions Gate Bridge) is seen under construction. The north shore, in the distance, will see a rise in population when the bridge is finished, but not as great as one might expect: the Great Depression still has us in its grip. Vancouver Public Library / 003033

It's the year 2001 and commuters are heading home to the north shore across the Lions Gate Bridge. The centre lane has a green light, designating the two north-bound lanes for the evening rush. In the morning, city-bound traffic will get the two lanes as seen in the photo at left.

A fabulous photograph from 1938 showing one of Canadian Pacific's Empress liners moving serenely into Burrard Inlet beneath the still-under-construction Lions Gate Bridge. There's plenty of room for the ship, with a 61-metre (200-foot) clearance between the water and the bridge deck. The total length of the bridge is 1,517.3 metres, or 4,978 feet.

Vancouver Public Library / 003035

No, the bridge hasn't shrunk. It is just that today's cruise ships have grown and this P&O liner is squeezing under the bridge to disembark its passengers at Canada Place.

Early stages of construction of the First Narrows Bridge looking from Stanley Park to the north shore, 1937
Vancouver Public Library / 003032

Workers place deck supports on the bridge. Construction had started on the substructure of the bridge in April 1937. This photograph was taken later that fall. City of Vancouver Archives / BR P24 N59#3

LIONS GATE BRIDGE

The initial proposal to build a bridge across the First Narrows was made in 1909, but rejected because of the impact the construction would have on Stanley Park. The Great Depression changed all that: the prospect of all those jobs to build the bridge was too tempting. Another reason for approval this time around: the bridge was, in effect, free. The Guinness Brewing Company had bought 4,000 acres on the north shore (at bargain-basement prices) and wanted to attract residents to its development there. Guinness paid for the bridge! Total cost: precisely $5,873,837.17.

When the provincial government bought the Lions Gate in 1963 it paid $6 million. A beautiful bargain.

Construction is well along in this 1938 view looking to the north. The bridge will open in November, and be dedicated by the visiting King George VI and Queen Elizabeth the following May. 33 Vancouver Public Library

When, on November 15, 1937, Premier Duff Pattullo took a welding torch and ceremoniously cut a chain-link barrier to open the New Westminster bridge named for him, he told the assembled throng it was a "thing of beauty." It does look rather attractive under construction… but nobody today calls this heavily-travelled bridge, with its scary, too-narrow mid-span bend, beautiful. One bumper sticker reads: I Drove the Pattullo… and Lived!

One of the proudest possessions of the New Westminster Museum is a huge model of the bridge made entirely of wood.   City of Vancouver Archives / BR P29 N75

A view south to the Pattullo Bridge, 2001.

A B.C. Electric trolley bus squeezes its way through the second Granville Street Bridge in 1953 while its much wider replacement, the current bridge, is under construction.
Vancouver Public Library / 082131

A view to the north with a now completed Granville Street Bridge at left. The Kids Market on Granville Island occupies space freed up when the old bridge was removed.

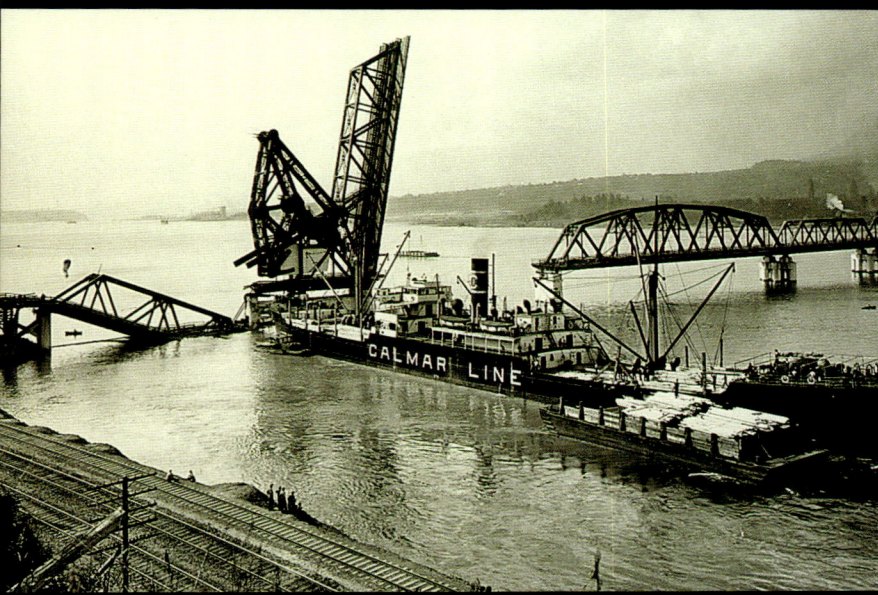

They called the old Second Narrows crossing the "Bridge of Sighs," because it was struck so often by ships. The lift span for the bridge was not mid-channel, but in the shallower waters nearer the north shore of the inlet. Big mistake. In the 1930 photograph above we see the Losmar of the Calmar Line, shortly after it struck the bridge and put it out of commission for months. Shortly after it reopened a barge got stuck underneath: the rising tide lifted the barge and you can guess what happened. It damaged the bridge so badly it was closed for four years. The ferries became extremely crowded. Vancouver Public Library / 002995

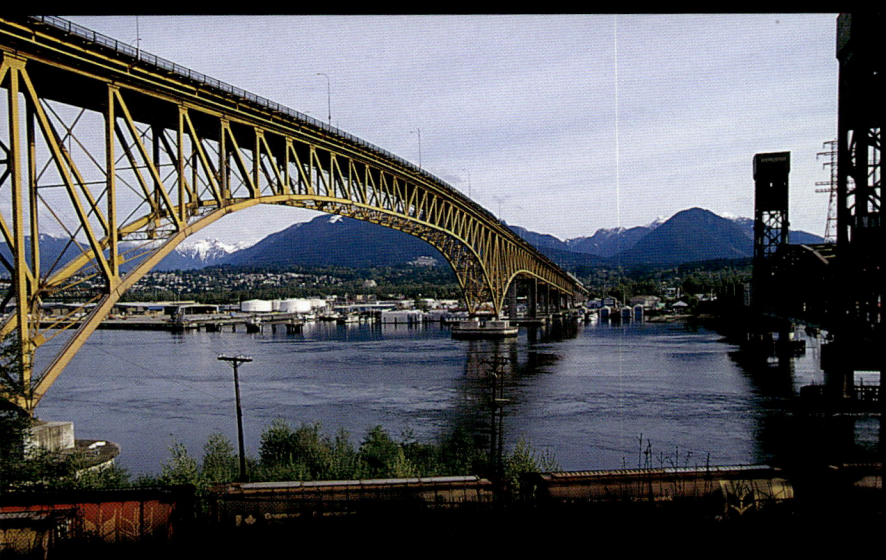

Second Narrows Bridge, 2001.

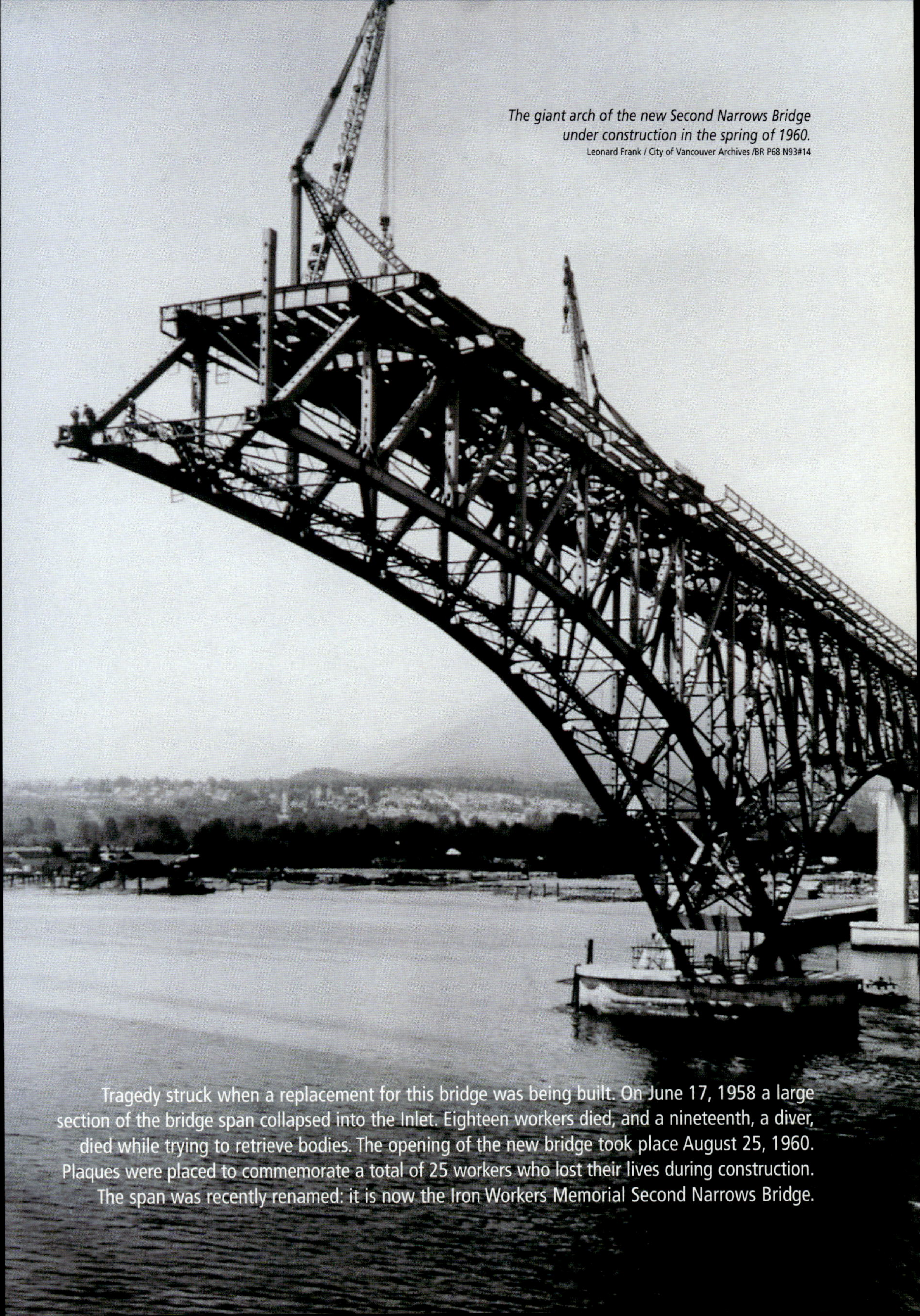

The giant arch of the new Second Narrows Bridge under construction in the spring of 1960.
Leonard Frank / City of Vancouver Archives /BR P68 N93#14

Tragedy struck when a replacement for this bridge was being built. On June 17, 1958 a large section of the bridge span collapsed into the Inlet. Eighteen workers died, and a nineteenth, a diver, died while trying to retrieve bodies. The opening of the new bridge took place August 25, 1960. Plaques were placed to commemorate a total of 25 workers who lost their lives during construction. The span was recently renamed: it is now the Iron Workers Memorial Second Narrows Bridge.

Aerial view of the Granville and Burrard bridges, 2001.

See the broad swath of flat land abutting the creek (just east of the north end of the bridge) in the old shots? That land would one day be the Expo 86 site. Today it's home to Concord Pacific's massive residential/commercial development visible at left. Vancouver Public Library / 082497

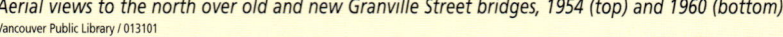

Aerial views to the north over old and new Granville Street bridges, 1954 (top) and 1960 (bottom).
Vancouver Public Library / 013101

The second and third Granville Street Bridges both show up in an early 1954 aerial photograph (upper right). The third and current Granville Street Bridge opened February 4, 1954, but it's not quite complete in the shot at top right: the wide southern portion visible in the lower 1960 shot, curving to align with Granville south of the bridge, is not yet built. The older bridge (it opened in 1909), visible beneath the current span in the 1954 shot, was demolished shortly after the new one opened. But, in a way, the old bridge lives on: steel plate girders taken from it were used in the construction of the foundations of yet another span, the Oak Street Bridge (1957).

In the 1954 photograph, Granville Island is still an island. It had been created from fill sucked from the bottom of False Creek, and from 1916 its 14.5 hectares became the city's industrial heart. So important was it during the Second World War that it was closed to the public for fear of saboteurs. By 1960, as you see, more fill had been added south of the island and it became a peninsula. Over the years industry began to move out and the "island" began to go downhill. Today Granville Island is home to a hugely successful public market, interesting restaurants and shops, and just enough industry to remind people of its former dominance in that role. It's one of the real success stories in the city's history.

View from Granville Street Bridge to the north west. A picturesque cloud bank frames the mountains on the north shore but the marina, Burrard Street Bridge and high-rises of the West End enjoy the summer sun. Here you see one reason Vancouver is frequently named as the most livable city in Canada.

Airside view of Vancouver 'International' in 1953. Note small Immigration and Customs shack at right and Trans Canada Airlines (TCA) DC-3 being gassed up on the ramp. Vancouver Public Library / 082133B

AIRPORT

The year after Charles Lindbergh made his famous solo flight across the Atlantic in May, 1927 he was touring American cities to talk about the future of aviation. When Lindbergh got to Seattle a Vancouver newspaper sent a reporter down. Asked if he would add Vancouver to his itinerary, the famous aviator replied; "No, there's no airport there fit to land on." Ouch. When that remark got back to Vancouver it spurred frantic activity, and a man named William Templeton was put in charge of getting an airport ready. His budget was minuscule, but he didn't let that stop him. When a well-known American airport design firm made an offer to design the complex, at a cost of several thousands of dollars, Templeton laughingly declined and did the work himself for about $14.

Some 55,000 people turned up for the airport's four-day opening ceremonies in 1931. By 1953 (above) the building of a brand-new three kilometre long, east-west runway earned the airport a Class A International standing. Now those DC-3s had lots of room to take off and land.

Aerial view looking east over a much expanded airport, C.l960. With the number of people strolling around the airliners we can assume an airshow is underway. Vancouver Public Library / 047903

Aerial view of the airport looking to the northwest from Richmond to the University of British Columbia on Point Grey, 2001.

Aerial view to the east over the airport, showing a predominantly pastoral Richmond, 1953. *Vancouver Public Library / 081144*

Aerial view to the north over Vancouver's first airport, 1931.
William Templeton / Vancouver Public Library / 013259

Two or three minutes and the new airport was on our left, a bleak, flat, dirty expanse of mud, broken by patches of disgusted-looking grass doing its best to soften the uninviting landscape. Then, a glance at the ripe-orange administration building, nearly completed, and the two candy stick hangars with their red-and-white stripes, transformed the drearily-hopeless scene into one of bright optimism and a promising future.

From "Afternoon Auto Ambles About Vancouver",
The VancouverSunday Province, 18 January 1931.

With the opening of the new International Terminal, the old facilities of the newly designated South Terminal were given over to cargo and charter operations.

One example of William Templeton's innovative and frugal ways can be found in the design of Cowley Crescent, the road that circled the little airport's first terminal. Templeton took a light bulb, placed it on the plan, and traced around it with a pencil. That was the road, and that's why Cowley Crescent has that shape to this day.

Aerial view over what is now called the South Terminal, once home to the main airport, toward Richmond across the Middle Arm of the Fraser River, 2001.

On the cockpit placard:

SEAT MUST BE IN
FORWARD 10 INCHES OF TRAVEL
DURING TAKEOFF AND LANDING

A sense of wonder is in itself a religious feeling. But in so many people the sense of wonder gets lost. It gets scarred over. It's as though a tortoise shell has grown over it. People reach a stage where they're never surprised, never delighted. They're never suddenly aware of glorious freedom or splendour in their lives. However hard a life may be, I think for virtually all people this is possible.

Robertson Davies, man-of-letters, interviewed by Alan Twigg in
Strong Voices: Conversations with Fifty Canadian Authors (1988).

Aerial view of the terminal area through wisps of British Columbia mist.

At the beginning of this section we showed Vancouver International Airport in 1953, a year when for the first time the airport handled more than 500,000 passengers. In 2000 there were 16.2 million, making this the second busiest airport in Canada and one of the great airports of the world. The Boeing 747 at left making its final approach to VIA is one of more than 500 aircraft either taking off or landing there every single day. A big new International Terminal Building opened in 1996, along with another three-kilometre runway, a dozen new interconnecting taxiways, extensions to existing taxiways and other amenities--along with state-of-the-art electronic landing guidance and lighting systems. (It's not just the planes that are coddled: recent expansion to the international terminal offers airport users glass-enclosed passenger boarding bridges to seven new gates, a walkway through a BC coastal forest landscape, and lots of outstanding local art work.)

Mr. Lindbergh? We're ready for you now!

Busy flight deck of a Boeing 747 as pilots line the giant machine up for landing at Vancouver Airport. Captain Ted Prinsen has his hands on the throttles, adjusting power for the final approach while First Officer Phil Tweten is handling radio communications and the checklists. The Arthur Laing Bridge, main runway and the Georgia Strait are all clearly visible through the Captain's windscreen.

VANDUSEN
BOTANICAL GARDENS

VanDusen Botanical Gardens, Vancouver.

NITOBE
MEMORIAL GARDEN

The Nitobe Memorial Garden, University of British Columbia.

We may paddle many moons on the sea, but our canoes will never enter the channel that leads to the yesterdays of the Indian people

Joe Capilano 1911

This is the lament of the Squamish chief who recounted his people's tales and traditions to the poet Pauline Johnson, who published them in her book Legends of Vancouver (1911).

EPILOGUE

That long white line above indicates the length of time we know people have been living in the lower mainland. It represents 8,000 years. The little colored blip at the end of the line represents the time covered by this book.

The life of the people who were here long before us (they have marked at least 80 centennials) is an interesting and complex story, and needs to be told in detail. Our more modest aim is to have looked at the years represented by *that* short yellow line.

It's a fascinating and colorful story. To look in these photographs at the proud steady gaze of the pioneering folk and the scattered shacks and wild, wandering roads of the earliest days, and to contrast them with the fast-paced, noisy, crowded and chaotic city we live and work in now is a sobering experience. We have gained much, but we have lost something, too. There was a gentleness and a calm slowness and a quieter tone to our earliest years that can never be recaptured.

Reliving them through the remarkable photographs of our past taken by pioneers like Leonard Frank, Philip Timms, Stuart Thomson, Claud Dettloff, Harry Devine, the Bailey Brothers and others is exhilarating and rewarding. Sometimes it seems inconceivable that a part of the city with which you're really familiar could once have looked like that.

The research into facts and photos has been great fun. It was aided immeasurably by the friendly and oh-so-informative people in the History Division at the Vancouver Public Library, and by the Library's Special Collections department… home to thousands of fascinating old photos. The City of Vancouver Archives have been an invaluable source of information for more than 60 years, and our book benefited tremendously from their holdings and their alert and hard-working staff. Thanks, too, to the North Vancouver Museum for their very friendly assistance.

Authors whose works provided valuable information include James Barr, Constance Brissenden, Rodger Burnes, Imbi Harding, Brian Kelly, Bruce Macdonald, Robert A.J. McDonald, Alex Matches, Major J.S. Matthews, Alan Morley, Eric Nicol, Sean Rossiter, Patricia Roy, Fred Thirkell, Robin Ward and many others… including numberless reporters of The Sun, the Province and earlier newspapers.

Here is 150 years of Vancouver and its surroundings. Step back into times gone by, and enjoy!

Chuck Davis, author
John McQuarrie, photographer and publisher